Touch in Schools

A revolutionary strategy for
replacing bullying with respect
and for reducing violence

Sylvie Hétu & Mia Elmsäter

Ur Publications & Programmes, Inc.

Montréal, Canada

MISSION STATEMENT

Ur Publications & Programmes Inc. wishes to bring to a wide readership, pioneering thinking at the leading-edge of evolving ideas within education, individual and social development, psychology and related fields – endeavouring to foster insight and creative impulses in these domains of human culture.

OUR UNDERTAKING

Ur Publications & Programmes Inc. guarantees to use a substantial proportion of its surplus to support cultural sphere activities, such as arts and education, according to Associative Economics principles.

For more information about Associative Economics, visit

www.ae-institute.com

UR
Publications &
Programmes Inc.

3937 rue St-hubert
Montréal, Qc Canada H2L 4A6

www.urpublications.com

First Published by Ur Publications & Programmes Inc. 2010
1st Edition 2010
2nd Edition 2013

International
hands-on respect

MISA   (Massage In Schools Association)
Registered Trademark 2002-MISA International

A catalogue record for this book is available from the British Library.

ISBN: 978-0-9736659-1-8

Cover photograph: Sylvie Hétu
Book design: Mark Miller ideas@brandnewcastle.com

Printed in the United Kingdom by PrintHouse Corporation, London
www.printhouse.co.uk

Dedication

To all the children ...
and especially to
the seven-year-old Swedish boy
who sparked the idea
behind this programme
by raising his hand at school
and asking:
"When's our massage?"

Acknowledgements

JOSEPH CHILTON PEARCE, SIR RICHARD BOWLBY, STEVE BIDDULPH, VIMALA MCCLURE, and SUE PALMER, for their generous endorsements of our book.

SYLVIA LINDGREN, who worked endless hours editing, reviewing, correcting, indexing, arguing, and putting her heart and soul into this book.

RICHARD HOUSE, who encouraged us to pursue our dream of Massage in Schools, gave us invaluable feedback and ideas for the book, and who gave time and care to editing and indexing.

MARK MILLER, our book designer, who took great pains to give coherent shape to our manuscript, scattered photographs, and quotations; and who has been highly respectful of and patient with our wishes, which he articulated very successfully and with great design skills.

AUTHOR SHELLEY MOSLEY, an experienced line editor and bibliography expert, who convinced us of the need for an index, and taught us a thing or three about punctuation and grammar – and who also convinced us that this book was worthy of being published.

DEBRA ZATELNY, who made available her great ability as a proof reader.

VIMALA MCCLURE, the founder of the global International Association of Infant Massage, and author of the book Infant Massage: A Handbook for Loving Parents, for which we have the utmost respect. It was through *Infant Massage* that the authors met, and through which we continue to gain further insight about the importance of touch in human beings' daily lives.

DR MARC LAFRANCE, from the Sociology Department of Concordia University, Montreal, Canada for his ongoing support and planned future research projects for the MISP.

ANDRÉE LANTHIER, who inspired us with ideas about movement for children.

GILL TREE, director of Essentials for Health, who organized the first Massage In Schools Programme (MISP) training, which took place in the UK.

DR MARGOT SUNDERLAND, director of the Centre for Child Mental Health in London, who saw the value of the MISP and offered to be an ambassador for the Massage In Schools Programme in England.

KAY WHITE, SHERON WILSMORE, KATE PIGEON-OWEN, ANNE CREASE, ANITA MORRIS, JEAN JOHNSON, MARY GANDER, and GLORIA WONG who sent in quotations from children, parents, and teachers.

CAROL TROWER, who 'took the bull by the horns' and was instrumental in getting the MISP started and up on its feet in the UK.

MATILDE BARBIER and ISABELLE NATALI, who helped organize photo shoots, and gave us valuable feedback from their experience with the programme.

ROD DAVIES, Head of Schools at Gibbs Green, EDWARD PEARSON-SHAUL, Special Educational Needs Co-ordinator (SENCO) at Tuckswood Community Primary School, and teacher KAREN ARMITAGE at Gibbs Green, who rescheduled classes and welcomed us to take photographs in their schools.

CHANTAL BÉLANGER, director of the school La Nacelle de Saint-Jean-Chrysostôme, who opened the doors of her school for the programme to be implemented and the photos taken; GINETTE NADEAU, who requested the programme in the school; and JENNIFER ARRUDA, who taught the strokes. CATHERINE TREMBLAY, the photographer; and PIERRE BLAIS, who coordinated the whole project for that school, and sent us comments from children.

MISP INSTRUCTORS IN PORTUGAL, and their willingness to be photographed during the 2007 MISP course.

DOUG REESE, who volunteered much time in helping us set up our first website and who demonstrated extraordinary patience with our limited knowledge of the process.

Our expert legal advisors... **ALAIN BERGERON**, **PIERRE PAQUIN**, and **STÉPHANIE THURBER**, who endlessly supported us in making this programme 'protected, sound, safe, and legal' for all involved parties.

A special thanks to **RICK FREESE**, President of Bookmasters, for his initial enthusiasm and trust in us, and to **DEB KEETS**, Vice President, Business Development of BookMasters, for her meticulous professionalism in regard to printing and distribution, for her faith in the project, and above all for her ongoing patience with our unremitting list of questions.

ALL INTERNATIONAL MISP TRAINERS AND INSTRUCTORS: we had the vision, and you are all now contributing to making it a reality.

PARENTS AND CHILDREN who kindly consented to letting us publish their pictures.

Our own children: **TIM**, **ERIK**, and **JOAKIM ELMSÄTER**, and **ETIENNE**, **JEAN-MICHEL**, and **JOANNIE HÉTU-GOSSARD**, who are our real teachers and advisors, often bringing us back down to earth and humbling us.

Our mums, **CASS** and **MONA**, who have been convinced that we live in airplanes in our efforts to spread nurturing touch all over the planet!

MICHAEL, who is there every time we ask for help... you are truly an angel!

Contents

Foreword

by Joseph Chilton Pearce

On visiting America years ago, Alfred Tomatis, the French physician whose pioneering research into hearing, speech, movement, and learning is a classic, remarked on the "touch-starved American child," by now an old story and far worse than in Tomatis' day. Today, as David Elkind recently pointed out, research into a child's neural-physical growth and development has extended our knowledge far beyond that of any previous generation, while we have miserably failed to apply any of this vast new research, even as the "crisis in childhood" grows daily.

The issue is: how do we, how can we, apply this vast array of new research? A dismaying flood of books relating to this subject and what to do about it is sent to me from many quarters, most hopelessly complex or over simplified, but, here, in this astonishingly thorough yet simple work lies the answer, one that stands out above the rest and calls out for a full response from all of us. This book, *Touch in Schools*, offers a wealth of critical information, given in so eminently simple, useful, and practical a form, that, when the equally simple answer-application is spelled out, one can only ask: Why hasn't this been done before?

The research and references given by Mia Elmsäter and Sylvie Hétu, drawing on a rapidly expanding field, are impressive, sound, and current. Above all, the application of this knowledge to the direct daily life of the child is brilliant, practical, and long overdue. Again and again we might wonder why this obvious, common-sense approach hasn't been thought of and applied before, although, of course, I find that variations of it have been employed for some time now by the Scandinavian countries – where they have the odd habit of listening to, observing, and applying what their scientists and child-research studies reveal.

Actually putting this practical program into the schools may face considerable challenge in the United States, Canada, Great Britain, and possibly other countries. Resistance may be high in those fundamentalist areas where pleasure is suspect and pain sanctified, where blind obedience is valued over true learning, to say nothing of happiness. The fact that the child learns, comprehends, and retains new information when the learning atmosphere is one of emotional coherency, nurturing, and care, can be lost in the backlash of ancient beliefs, myths, superstitions, and inherited misconceptions.

While the following information is remarkably thorough to be so brief and succinct, I take the liberty of adding an all-too-brief mention of one relevant item from the two decades of heart–brain research taking place at The Institute of HeartMath. There, stunning and extensive research graphs show the "electricity of touch" which is eminently applicable to those aspects of child-and-school covered here. When people touch each other in simple gestures of friendliness, the electro-magnetic fields produced by their brains go into synchronous coherence with the e-m fields of their hearts. The overlapping of two such coherent fields strengthens the coherent orderliness of both persons' heart–brain systems, moving them toward a unity of mind, heart, and body integral to learning and creativity, and is the very fabric of social bonding.

In this state of heart–brain coherency, relationships are silently established and strengthened, new learning can take place without stress, a feeling of calm can prevail which profoundly affects people of all ages. Linking HeartMath's findings with the corresponding practice of touch offered here, offers a happy, productive, and powerful union.

To claim that an ecology of peace, the possibility for actually bringing our world into a coherent and harmonious state, is inherent within this simple solution offered in Touch in Schools seems extreme, but our situation is extreme and new solutions are called for. The ecology of the child and the earth are intricately interwoven, and both systems are in grave need of a different response from those of us involved, which means, of course, every single one of us. May we all give thanks to Elmsäter and Hétu for their pioneering efforts, and support them in every possible way. I am honoured and indeed flattered to have been asked, here in my 82nd year, for my response to this remarkable book, and only wish I were younger, with a bit more time and energy left, to work for such a cause.

Joseph Chilton Pearce

Author:

The Crack in the Cosmic Egg

Exploring the Crack in the Cosmic Egg

Magical Child

The Bond of Power (Spiritual Awakening)

Magical Child Matures (Magical Child-Magical Teen)

Evolution's End

The Biology of Transcendence

The Death of Religion and Rebirth of Spirit –
Rediscovering the Intelligence of Heart

"…we need to break through
the present taboo and
take cognisance of
the human need for
the reassurance of contact."

Jean Liedloff

The Continuum Concept

Introduction:
When Children Shoot Children

*"Too often we underestimate the power of a touch, a smile,
a kind word, a listening ear, an honest compliment,
or the smallest act of caring, all of which have
the potential to turn a life around."*

Leo Buscalgia

When children shoot each other, we as adults have a problem. It is tempting to think that shootings occur in other schools, in other cities, in other countries, and that they could never happen in our own neighbourhoods. However, in some very important sense, we are collectively responsible. This is a challenge everyone must face.

There are many crises in education and schooling systems worldwide, crises which are manifesting in different ways – for example, more children than ever are becoming depressed, and at younger and younger ages, precipitating an escalation in child and teenage suicides, and in dropout rates. Violence, in the form of bullying, school exclusion, and disrespect for teachers, is also increasing dramatically. Learning disabilities, like hyperactivity and Attention Deficit Disorder, are additional examples of problems which are on the increase.

As the authors of this book, we are committed to facing these challenges, and with this book we offer a positive proposal for improving the quality of children's everyday experiences in schools. Though *Touch in Schools* does not promise to resolve all of the aforementioned crises and their accompanying malaise, we are confident that it can change matters substantially for the better. The field of education is in need of major transformation in order to meet the true needs of our children, and the programme described in this book is a major yet easily achievable step in the right direction.

The proposal presented in this book is centred on powerful, life-giving touch and movement, organized and delivered within the modern school setting. The respectful touch at the core of the programme takes the simple form of children massaging each other. The Massage In Schools Programme (MISP) gives children a welcome opportunity to pause and take a breath. Hopefully, it will also encourage everyone involved in education to pause, and in the process to rediscover and re-clarify the deep meaning of raising, educating, and caring for children and their needs.

In short, the MISP proposes the widespread, or even universal, introduction and embedding of *positive touch and movement* into the school curriculum and into school activities more generally. We maintain that movement and touch are necessary for children's healthy learning and well being, just as water, air, and food are also necessary for their growing bodies.

"The human being would never become conscious of the divine without the sense of touch."

Rudolf Steiner

11

1. Toward social change

"Why must we reinvent education now?
The too short answer is:
for decent human survival."

Gary McIntyre Boyd

Change does not happen overnight. It is well known that it takes many years (some historians say at least 50 years) to change cultural habits. It also takes the participation of a certain percentage of a given population for a sustainable shift in collective beliefs to occur. With the Massage In Schools Programme, we are making a considerable contribution to the cultural shift that will enable increasing numbers of children to experience a pro-touch society. We intend this programme to contribute toward a new social order, where values such as compassion and respect will emerge from healthy attitudes toward touch.

People relate to each other through, by, in, with, and from their physical bodies. The denial of physical touch can lead to subtle isolation, unbalanced individualism, and diminished social abilities. One consequence of the lack of consciously developed positive touch within education may be burgeoning levels of disrespect, as well as the abuse of our bodies, be it self-abuse or the abuse of others. Society needs to re-educate itself both collectively and individually in relation to touch, in order to bring about a better society. Touch benefits us from birth to death – and re-education is certainly necessary.

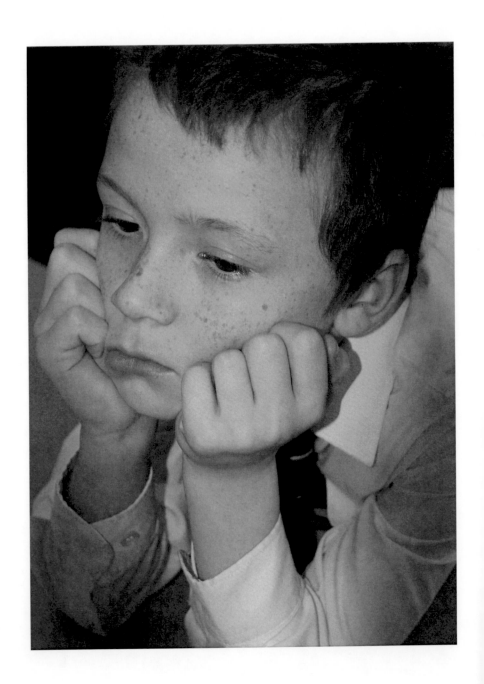

2. Education is in Trouble

"Today's children are, literally, losing their interest in their subjects, their interest in their teachers, their interest in school, and their interest in life itself [...]
They lack the soul forces that could generate interest, and so they become ever more passive and poor in spirit."

Eugene Schwartz

If we were to count the number of trees that have been cut down to produce the paper on which reports, analyses, statistical data, and curriculum reforms on education have been printed, it would surely be a shocking figure! Whilst we should and do honour all honest attempts that are made to help children thrive in schools, the manifold negative symptoms that are commonly observed in modern schooling systems can leave us blank and incredulous. What is it that children, through their behaviour, are trying to communicate to their educators and teachers? Why is it that so many children do not thrive? Why is it that so few children seem to really fit in and succeed within the existing mainstream educational system? Why does the current educational system suit only a certain category of children, but seem to fail the majority?

We simply cannot ignore the fact that many children are suffering in the modern schooling system. The escalating rates of violence, truancy and dropouts, exclusion, bullying, and suicide are indicators of a general malaise that children, worldwide, are manifesting. This results in teachers burning-out and social workers being overloaded with more and more cases.

Notwithstanding the noble efforts of teachers, psycho-educators, educational psychologists, psychiatrists, psychotherapists, counsellors, and parents, education is noticeably still in deep trouble.

So where did we miss the boat?

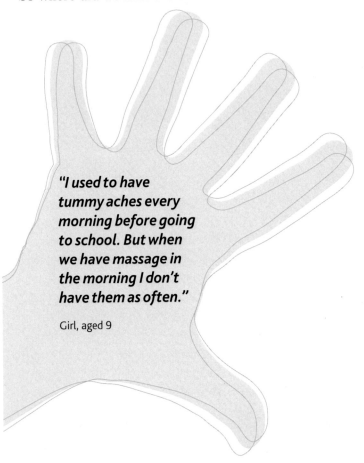

"I used to have tummy aches every morning before going to school. But when we have massage in the morning I don't have them as often."

Girl, aged 9

3. Simply Simple

"There is but one temple in the universe, and that is the Body of Man. Nothing is holier than that high form. Bending before man is a reverence done to this Revelation of the Flesh. We touch heaven when we lay our hands on a human body."

Novalis

We wish to emphasize that this book and approach will not solve the global crisis in education. However, our years of experience in working with parents and babies, children and teachers, have led us to an interesting conclusion: as human beings, we tend to complicate things that are simple.

Over the past century, modernity has brought extraordinary innovations to society that our great-grandparents could never have imagined. Yet we can certainly question whether our life has really become simpler with the introduction of cars, dishwashers, and the like. Whether or not we are more evolved as a species as a result of computers, airplanes, and television remains, in our view, an open question.

Without being simplistic, we believe in simplicity. We also believe that the human nervous system, especially where babies and children are concerned, may well be on "overload" with too much stimulation. It is well known that many children in the modern world are both over- and under-stimulated. The kind of stimulation that a child experiences from the time he wakes up until he arrives at school could well be of a similar magnitude to the stimulation his grandmother might have experienced during an entire month of her life!

The question then arises: What is it, simply, that children need? This in turn brings us back to what is essential. In order to grow, children need to be kept warm, to have food, and to be loved. They can then learn, and find their place in the world.

While we cannot go back to the past, we are suggesting that there is a need for a return to healthy simplicity. The introduction of healthy touch and movement in schools is one step in that direction.

"I like getting massaged."

Boy, aged 5

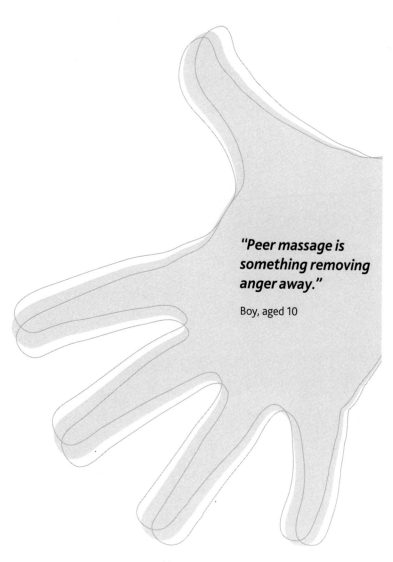

"Peer massage is something removing anger away."

Boy, aged 10

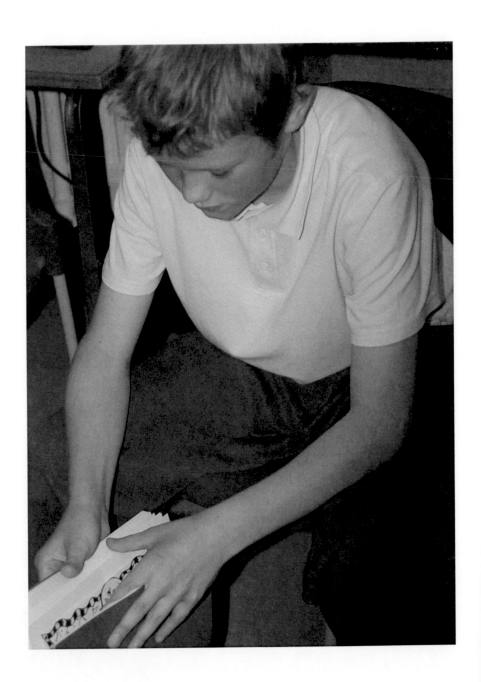

4. No Time?

"Humans have an insatiable appetite for knowledge and invention aimed at making their life better and easier. However, our genetically inherited developmental needs remain unchanged. If we allow them to be submerged by the lifestyle that technological and social progress has made available, we get into trouble."

Sir Richard Bowlby

The acceleration of time

In a radio interview, a child was asked what he wanted to do during the school vacation. To that, he replied, "Nothing. I want a vacation."

More and more children are suffering from depression. We suspect they are overwhelmed by the high expectations to which they have to respond. Adults now want so much for children that they strive to provide them with every possible opportunity, right from the beginning. The ironic result is that children sometimes have an even bigger load on their schedule than their parents have!

There are different courses they can attend, computer games to play, an entire host of TV programmes and films to watch, various after-school programmes and sporting activities in which to participate, music to listen to, friends to chat with… and then there is the homework they have to do in the evening. A school curriculum defines specific goals and targets to which they need to conform, and with which they must integrate at a pre-determined rate. Add to that all the examinations, tests, and evaluations, and it is easy to understand why today's children can often feel overwhelmed.

Where has the time actually gone? Their parents and teachers, caught up in their own life, professional expectations, and schedules, teach children to also get caught up in the spiralling "no time" syndrome. Of course, some end up simply burning out. In such an environment, how can children learn to relax and just breathe? When and where can they just play? Where is the spontaneous laughter of children, re-inventing the world in their games and play?

The scientist, philosopher, and educationalist Rudolf Steiner, founder of Waldorf education, maintains that "play is the work of young children", and that education should always be approached with the rhythmical image of "breathing in and breathing out". There needs to be a balance between what children take in, and the time it takes to integrate what they absorb. The rhythmical image can be viewed as a dance between the *intellectual* activities of taking in something new and the *physical* activities of integrating the same. The whole body needs to be considered in this process, including resting certain parts of the body/mind while others are active. Resting means more than just morning or afternoon breaks. Resting the mind by doing, for example, a touch activity is a way for integration to take place. Rhythm needs to be an integral part of daily life at school.

We strongly believe that those of us who are responsible for children's education need to reconsider the use of time, and how to distribute the various activities we bring to them. Many teachers have told us, "We just don't have time to incorporate touch, massage, and movement into our day because the curriculum is already too packed". This reveals to us the severity of our loss of common sense regarding the use of time with children.

"I like doing peer massage. I like going to school and now I have lots of friends. I think better and my teacher is nice."

Girl, aged 9

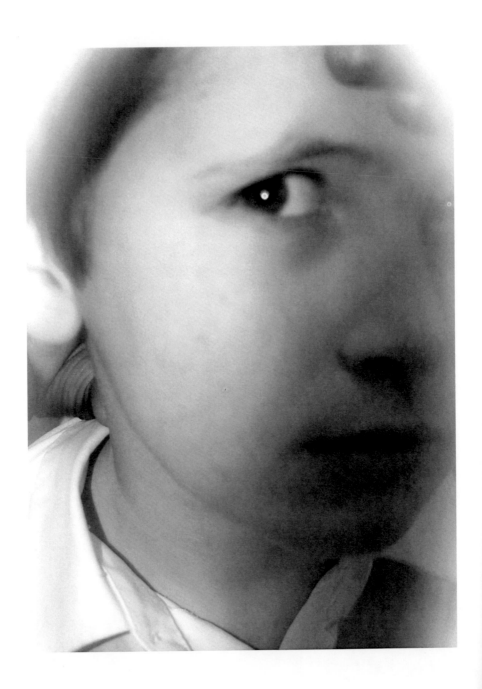

5. Children: Who are they?

"Children and young people are naturally disposed towards a playful approach to life and it does them good to share this with their adults, who have all too often put away childish things. It is well known that a period of relaxation will enable people to come refreshed to whatever task they are involved in, so a break for spontaneous play can prove beneficial in any situation."

Mildred Masheder

Children: who are they? That could well be a deep philosophical question. Philosophers and psychologists still engage in age-old debates about human nature, human development, and human beings per se. It is an intrinsic part of human nature to look for answers and we are enthusiastic in our desire to understand who we are, and how we become adult human beings.

We identify, classify, and describe stages with precision, trying to find the golden thread of what is common to us all. At the same time, we embrace what is unique in the individual, which can easily bring up opposing and seemingly contradictory views. Is it environment, food, culture, parents, schooling, or genetics that shapes a child? While it is true that all of these factors play a part in shaping the individual, mystery still surrounds what makes each human being unique. Various studies have been carried out on identical twins who were mysteriously different right from the start. However, we are convinced that there is one constant – *that a baby, a child, needs other human beings to become human.* Children who were abandoned in forests and raised by animals usually do not learn to walk on two feet, learn a language, nor learn social skills.

It is clear that education is necessary, and human interaction crucial. However, it must be acknowledged that the way humans interact with one another as adults is different from the kind of interaction that a child needs. This is where the constant quest for understanding of how we as human beings develop, and what is fundamentally needed at each stage, remain valid fields of research.

Our experience has led us to the conclusion that the main way in which we commonly teach and educate children is based too much on the way adults think, rather than on the way *children* think. It is as if we were trying systematically to incorporate adult thinking and knowledge into a child, in a pre-decided, sequentially agreed-upon process, including what each child should master at each age or each grade. We believe that we would all gain by trying to further develop knowledge about children and how we, as educators, can, in a responsible way, readjust our adult thinking to their child thinking.

This is a subtle issue. What we are maintaining here does not in any way mean that children should tell adults what they need. Children do not yet possess the developmental maturity to do so in an objective, informed way. They are still too immersed in experiencing life to be able to contemplate reflectively on who they are and then describe it. This latter ability is an adult way of thinking. However, it is our responsibility to find appropriate ways of caring for and educating our children, without necessarily expecting them to articulate their needs in words.

When education is too orientated toward the way adults think, it leads to a situation where many children find themselves struggling to figure out individual ways of learning, and that effort is far from respected and understood. Moreover, many other children simply cannot find the space to develop and learn in an individual way, thereby hampering their overall educational development.

Professor Howard Gardner has brought to the fields of psychology and education the idea of multiple intelligences, showing that each individual has certain strengths in their way of understanding the world. The role of educators should be to: first, thoroughly understand the different kinds of intelligences; secondly, develop the ability to find appropriate ways of educating (all forms of intelligences); and last but not least, become experts in identifying how each child learns. Thus, the educator would constantly be researching and studying child development, and constantly observing and identifying each child's uniqueness in order to find appropriate methodologies.

Generally speaking, mainstream education is based on language and logic, which merely reaches perhaps 20 per cent of children. What happens to the other 80 per cent? They simply do not thrive. Of course, there are many alternative schools, with strengths and weaknesses, that are attempting to find other ways to educate children with respect for their deep nature and their various learning styles. There is still a great deal to be discovered about this subject, but in the mean time, many children are still suffering.

Careful and common-sense observation of children clearly shows us that they are not "miniature adults", but developing human beings. Before they become adults, children are children, and they should be respected as such. Children, for example, are much more engaged in bodily movement than are adults. Adults, by contrast, are much more involved in thinking than they are in movement. Although we are in our body and relate to the world with our senses, our adult thinking activity is very different from the spontaneous play, movement, and imagination of the child. It is both interesting and revealing that when a child is about 4 years old, we as adults can have the child sit down and teach her to read (a very symbolic thinking activity), and value that much more than we value free imaginative play. That we value reading more highly could in part be attributed to our separation from the world of children, and in part to the prevailing general socio-cultural values in the modern world. The adult world values work more than play or what we call "leisure/recreational activities". Perhaps we all have a less-than-conscious anxiety that our children will not be able to work and be successful once they reach adulthood.

Have we forgotten what it is to be a child? We have forgotten that play, for a child, is a totally different world, and it is necessary and essential for his healthy development. We have forgotten that when a child uses his imagination, he strengthens his social and intellectual skills. We have forgotten that the great scientist Albert Einstein learned to read at a very late stage in his own childhood, and yet he became one of the towering geniuses of modern science. We have come to incorrectly believe that if a child reads at four, she will succeed in life. In short, we have forgotten what it is to be a child.

It could take many years before we fully understand the impact of modern teaching approaches on children's learning, behaviour, and self-esteem. For fundamental reform to occur in education, reform that will truly address all our children, it will demand of us the courage to revisit the real question of children: "Who are they?".

The Massage In Schools Programme (hereafter referred to by its acronym, MISP) is proposing one stepping-stone toward the day when all children can naturally find their place in school. This is because MISP addresses important fundamental needs of all human beings, needs that go beyond culture and beliefs: positive touch and human interaction.

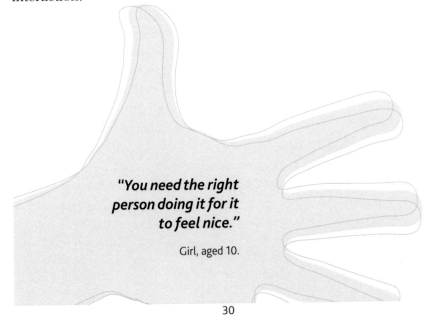

"You need the right person doing it for it to feel nice."

Girl, aged 10.

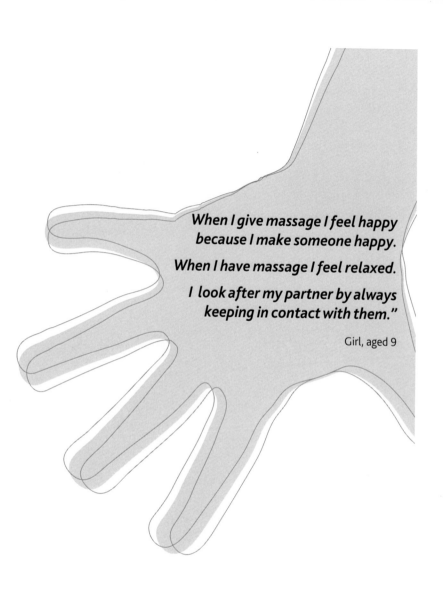

When I give massage I feel happy because I make someone happy.

When I have massage I feel relaxed.

I look after my partner by always keeping in contact with them."

Girl, aged 9

"Inculcating the values of
a new society – a postmodern society
– demands that education
be open-ended, life enhancing,
and growth oriented."

Raymond Petit

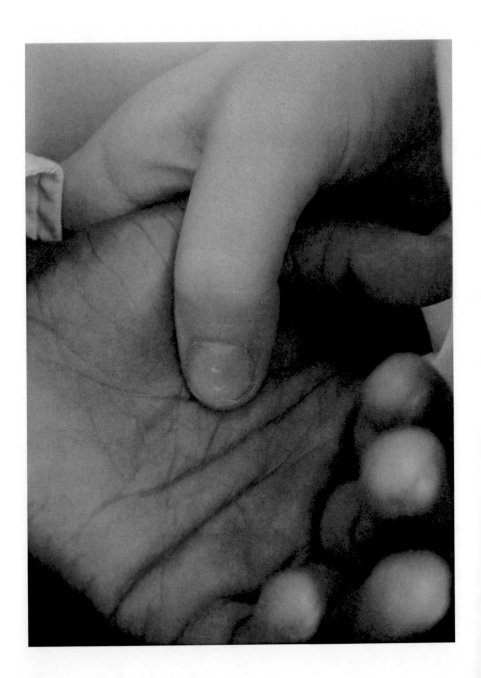

6. The Sense of Touch

"The skin, the flexible, continuous caparison of our bodies, like a cloak covers us all over. It is the oldest and the most sensitive of our organs, our first medium of communication, and our most efficient protector."

Ashley Montagu

The late, well-known author Ashley Montagu states in his book *Touching* that human beings cannot survive without touch. His statement is based on years of study and research data about human history in relationship to touch. Although the book was written some years ago now, its insights are still being supported by numerous studies from biologists, psychologists, physiologists, and neuroscientists.

Why, then, is touch still so taboo in so many societies? No-touch or minimal touch policies have even been implemented in our schools. Why? Many teachers have told us how confused they are about those policies. If a young child is hurting, the teachers may not even be allowed to comfort them with touch. We should remember the distressing studies that were conducted in which babies and children were deprived of loving, nurturing touch. Based on the many studies cited in his book, Montagu describes the devastating results – that they either died, or developed severe social and behavioural problems.

Touch is our most important sense. It is the first sense to be developed *in utero*, and the last one to leave us before we die. We cannot survive without it.

The sense of touch works through our skin with various receptors connected to nerves where information travels toward the brain, and finally gets interpreted. These sophisticated receptors fall into different categories with specific tasks, allowing us to feel pain, heat, cold, pressure, and texture. Thus, they allow us to receive constant direct sensorial information about the world around us.

Some areas of our bodies have high concentrations of touch receptors, such as our hands and lips; while in other areas the touch receptors are further apart. For example, the receptors on our back are further apart, which can provide an explanation as to why people feel more comfortable having their backs touched. Consider also the concept that we learn a great deal about someone just by shaking hands. Touch teaches us about people, but it also teaches us about the world. The truth is we cannot live without touch.

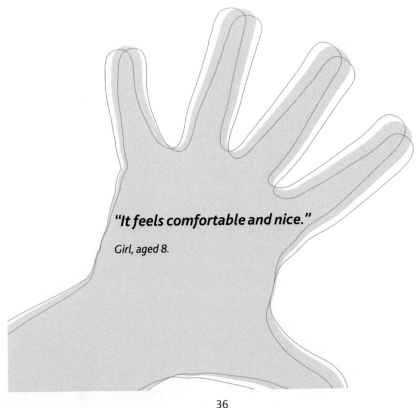

"It feels comfortable and nice."

Girl, aged 8.

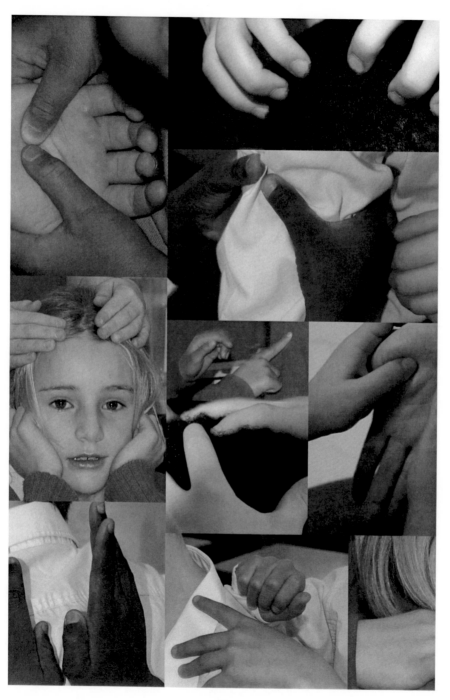

37

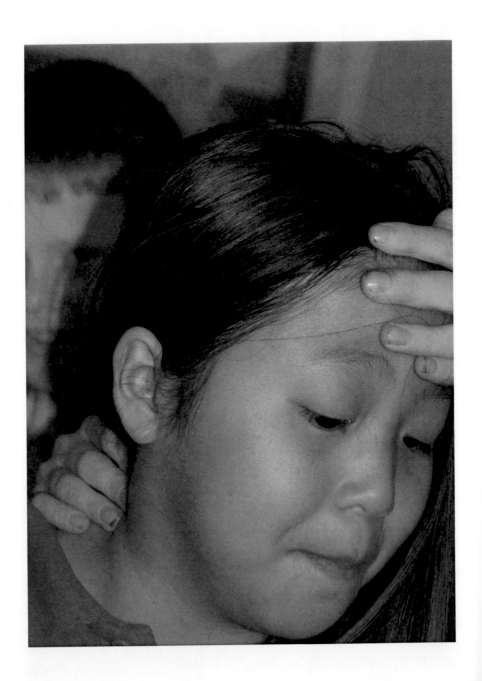

7. Touch and Culture

"…the touch-starved American child […] has never
received enough emotional or physical nurturing.
We must understand here that the emotional and physical are
essentially the same. So many American teenagers today have been
deprived of touch and love from the very beginning of their lives."

Joseph Chilton Pearce

An interesting study conducted by Sidney Jourard in the 1960s showed how often people from four culturally different countries touched each other. He observed the number of times pairs of people touched each other during a period of one hour in coffee shops. The surprising results were as follows:

- in San Juan, Puerto Rico, an average of 180 times an hour
- in Paris, France, an average of 110 times an hour
- in Gainesville, Florida, USA, only twice an hour
- in London, England, they didn't touch each other at all!

Some cultures are more touch oriented than others, as people having lived in or travelled to various countries can easily confirm. As individuals, we all have a certain relationship with touch itself, based on our personality, how we were raised, and the culture surrounding us.

When people live in a non-tactile society, their reactions to massage, especially in relation to children, are often met with suspicion.

Unfortunately, children and their bodies are still abused today. At any time, we can read in the newspapers about paedophiles, incest, and sexual abuse; so it is not uncommon for people to be sceptical about, or wary of, introducing massage into the schools.

Although we would all like to ensure that our children will never be abused, sexually or otherwise, it is ultimately impossible to provide a 100 per cent guarantee. What we can give them, however, is a safe and secure understanding of touch. When children touch each other in a loving way, through giving and receiving massage, the chances are greater that the child will do everything possible to avoid situations in which adults approach them with inappropriate erotic intentions.

There are certainly differences between cultures regarding touch. However, there still seems to be a lack of conscious understanding of the importance of touch, and therefore a lack of conscious investigation into the use of touch in child-rearing and education.

No matter to which culture we belong or in which culture we were raised, the importance of addressing touch as a fundamental aspect of human development seems crucial in the light of objective discoveries, both from the scientific and the psychological/psychiatric fields.

Conscious education about touch in general, and touch within education in particular, goes beyond cultures. Touch is important, regardless of culture.

"We are moving and I just found out that they have massage in schools in my new school. I feel so much better about moving."

Girl, aged 12

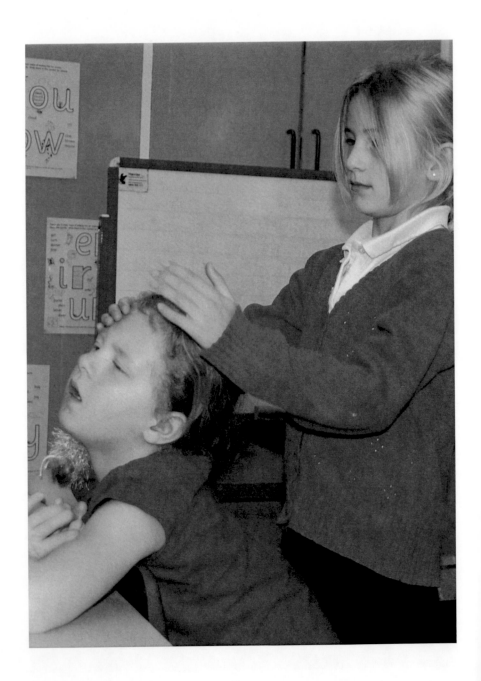

8. An Oxytocin Kick

*"The oxytocin that good relationships produce
is our personal healing nectar."*

Dr Kerstin Uvnäs-Moberg

Oxytocin has always been seen as the hormone that is released with birth and breast-feeding the baby. In 1906, an English researcher, Sir Henry Dale, discovered that there was a substance in the hypophysis (pituitary gland), which helped women give birth more quickly. He called this substance oxytocin, which originates from the Greek language and means "quick birth".

While oxytocin assists with the entire birth, helping with the contraction of the uterus after birth and with the start of lactation in nursing mothers, it does much more than that in our body. It is also known as the hormone that is implicated in feelings of well-being.

The Oxytocin Factor

The Oxytocin Factor: Tapping the Hormone of Calm, Love, and Healing is the title of a book written by Swedish researcher, Dr Kerstin Uvnäs-Moberg, who researched the effects of oxytocin. Being one of the leading experts on the subject, she is a strong supporter of the massage in schools concept. Her book is very reader-friendly, and anyone interested in knowing more about the science behind oxytocin, as well as the effects of touch, will gain much from reading it.

A hormone and a brain transmitter

According to the *Dorland's Medical Dictionary for Health Consumers*, "A hormone is a chemical substance produced in the body which has a specific regulatory effect on the activity of certain cells or a certain organ or organs". Oxytocin is not only a hormone; it also works as a type of transmitter, or signal substance in the brain. There are two types of oxytocin produced in the hypothalamus. The oxytocin that is produced in the larger cells is sent to the hypophysis, and from there goes out in the blood, functioning as a hormone. The oxytocin produced in the smaller cells goes out to other portions of the brain, functioning as a transmitter that affects the autonomic system and other regulating systems.

Oxytocin can be an answer to the fact that anguish, depression, and stress-related illnesses can be minimized through touch – and that the experience resulting from its release in the body leaves one feeling good.

Research and studies

Although research on oxytocin is still on-going, the findings are very promising. The information provided by Dr Kerstin Uvnäs-Moberg is very important in the context of massage. One interesting aspect is that a person watching someone else receiving a massage will often display similar calming benefits as the person who actually experiences the massage. We know that oxytocin is released into the body of a person receiving massage; however, it may be surprising to learn that oxytocin is also being released into the body of the person watching the massage. Uvnäs-Moberg is studying a possible subtle effect of oxytocin on the vomeronasal organ. Her research indicates that this organ may be able to detect oxytocin.

The vomeronasal organ (VNO or Jacobson's organ) is a chemo-receptor organ located between the nose and the mouth, but its function is still somewhat mysterious. The VNO has long been known to be present in human foetuses and has been reported sporadically in adults since the eighteenth century. The sensory neurons within the vomeronasal organ detect distinct chemical compounds and there is evidence of chemosensory communication in humans, as in the synchronization of menstrual cycles among women who live together.

Whether this organ plays a part in detecting oxytocin in human beings is yet to be determined, but it is clear that even children who neither want to be massaged nor to give massage still benefit from the massage that they watch. This phenomenon has been observed by several MISP Instructors as well as by school teachers.

Oxytocin in the classroom

Understanding that watching children massage each other can produce a positive effect on the observer is also valuable when working with the programme, and class teachers themselves will also benefit.

Studies and research projects have now confirmed that oxytocin is released in the body of the person who is gently touched, as well as in the person who is gently giving the touch. Thus, with oxytocin levels in our brain being raised by just watching, this means that the teacher, as well as any student/pupil who did not wish to give or receive massage that day, will feel the effects from just watching.

Oxytocin in each child

If we think about the effects of oxytocin within each child, we can easily make links with some of the previously mentioned benefits and we can easily understand that oxytocin can lead to a number of benefits, such as improved levels of attention, self-esteem, calmness, respect, and a reduction in aggression and violence.

As adults, we understand that it is not healthy for us to become over-stressed. We have an excellent opportunity to teach children how to do something good for themselves each morning before school begins. Taking the opportunity to let oxytocin take over for a few minutes in the classroom will truly help everyone to begin the day feeling calmer, relaxed, and positive, thereby enhancing the entire atmosphere for learning and higher social skills during each day at school.

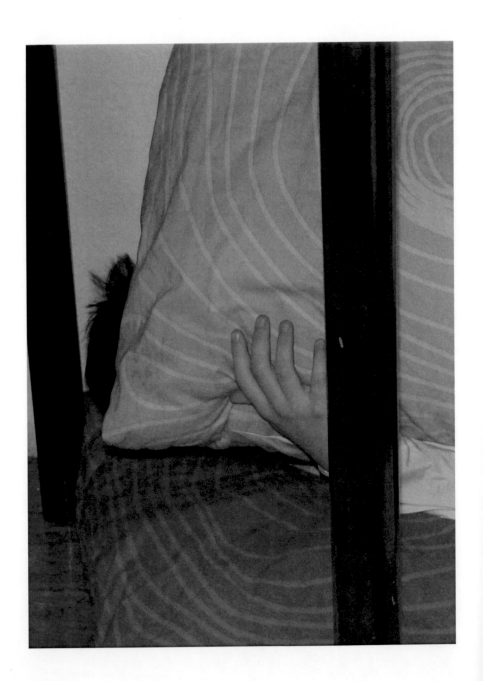

9. Fight or Flight

"Children increasingly pay a price for leading rushing lives. Kids as young as five now suffer from upset stomachs, headaches, insomnia, depression and eating disorders brought on by stress."

Carl Honoré

Our sensitive nervous system

As human beings, we are at a very interesting point in our evolution, as science begins to reveal some secrets about us. Our brain and our nervous system are under the metaphorical magnifying glass, and they are proving to be fascinating. In relation to our programme, we are interested in understanding how the nervous system as well as the brain reacts to touch and to the environment.

We experience the world with all of our senses, which are constantly sending messages to the brain via our nervous system. Based on the type of stimuli received by our senses, nerves start to create pathways, which in turn activate the brain. It seems important to state here that research is discovering that a child's nervous system can be *under-stimulated*, leading to learning difficulties, as well as to behavioural, emotional, and social challenges. Interestingly enough, being over-stimulated can lead to the very same problems. We believe that our frenetic hyper-modern culture is generating the phenomenon of over-stimulation, the effects of which are also being underestimated.

The entire process is very subtle. Starting from our own point of view, we can easily appreciate the fact that sometimes we have too much going on and feel overwhelmed, and at times it can also leave us feeling deprived. We observe the very same phenomena in children. Whilst adults are responsible for themselves and can take appropriate action, it is the responsibility of educators to establish parameters that will enhance children's ability to cope with the experiences they encounter.

Children who are overwhelmed

If we compare life, say, 50 years ago to life now at the beginning of the third millennium, it is all too easy to see that everything moves at a much faster pace. Modernity has brought many advantages and comforts to society in many countries, but it has also brought some disadvantages and discomforts. Materialism, competition, performance, and over-consumption have woven their way into the day-to-day lives of children, and into the very fabric of our human existence. There are more colours, fast-moving vehicles, food, music, sounds, toys, video games, DVDs, etc., to name just a few of the phenomena of modernity. With the appearance of all these manifold stimulants, there has been a steep increase in the number of children diagnosed with problems such as Attention Deficit Disorder and hyperactivity around the world, and this phenomenon is rapidly becoming an endemic challenge for all educators and policy-makers. Interestingly enough, the prevalence of autism, anorexia, and suicide has also begun to burgeon.

So what is it that we are missing here?

Reactions

"Fight or flight" reactions come from the lower part of the brain and are more primitive reactions, in which the more highly evolved part of the brain is not involved. Children can and do react to a specific stimulus in a specific moment, or can develop long-term reactions to continual stimuli. When the nervous system is taken by surprise, fight or flight reactions are likely to occur. A conclusion can be drawn that many modern-day children receive improper stimuli in relation to their capabilities, leading to a constant and often chronic overloading of their developing nervous system. This in turn leads to the slower development of the higher brain, in order that it can play its proper role – ultimately leading to undesirable reactions in children, both immediate and long term.

Protecting the nervous system

Many people who actively work within the field of education believe that children must be protected from an over-stimulating environment. Parents and teachers are encouraged to consider, as educators, the fact that they should play a strong role in choosing for their children the proper environment and appropriate stimuli for their healthy development. Far too many children have too much of everything, and not enough of the essentials, such as human contact, outdoor activities, eye contact, and so on. Whilst children often have too many toys and objects, and too many activities, they often lack simple human interactions with the people they cherish. This programme could easily have become a contraindication to its own intention, if it had not been developed with acute awareness and determination to educate children in a protected ambience which is respectful of their sometimes fragile and nurturing nature.

Massage and the nervous system

The good news about massage is that it activates our parasympathetic nervous system, the part of our autonomic nervous system which is responsible for our experiencing a sense of peace, calmness, and relaxation. When the parasympathetic system is well activated, we also digest our food more successfully and assimilate vitamins and minerals more effectively. In contrast, our sympathetic nervous system helps us in stressful situations, which, unfortunately, is called upon all too often in and by modern lifestyles.

Gentle massage is beneficial to the nervous system and has a positive effect on children. There is an interesting phenomenon that many people have already experienced in the practice of, for example, exercise, dance, tai chi, or yoga; it is a feeling of total relaxation yet, at the same time, acute attention and alertness. This is true for children receiving gentle massage as well – they become alert and able to pay attention and concentrate more.

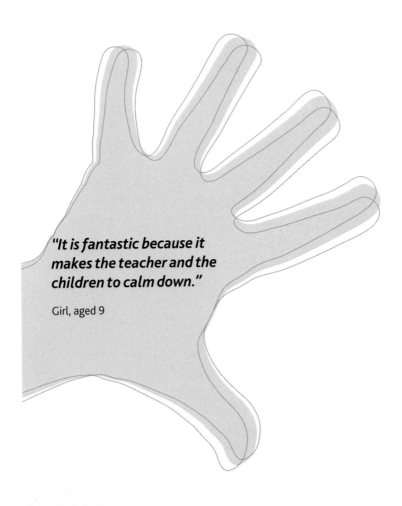

"It is fantastic because it makes the teacher and the children to calm down."

Girl, aged 9

*"If I don't feel like massage,
I can say no."*

Girl, aged 7

10. Ways of Learning

....

*"The more one can build an element of play – of fun,
of enjoyment – into learning experiences,
the better the learning will be."*

James Hemming

....

Rudolf Steiner, along with several modern researchers, warns educators about the dangers of prematurely bringing intellectual work to young children, as this has a negative impact on their development and impairs their learning abilities. A child must encounter the world step by step, and during the first seven years, he should primarily use imagination, imitation, and movement to integrate the world.

Some neuroscientists have discovered that bringing a child into abstract thinking too early has the ironic effect of diverting the child from crucial aspects of cognitive development. Premature intellectual activity can actually put too many developmentally inappropriate demands on the brain. Children need to get to know their bodies before understanding what is inside their heads. Learning to think abstractly will be far more profoundly integrated if experienced at a later, developmentally appropriate stage. If children are brought too much into their heads, their bodies can have unconscious and direct reactions that can range from high sensitivity to extreme apathy. The "available energy" is incorrectly channelled, and the child unconsciously tries to balance it, one way or the other, which is often misinterpreted as "wrong" behaviour.

Our adult mentality highly values the intellect – and rightly so! However, too many national educational curricula seem to have misunderstood the specificities of how *children* learn and develop. For so many children, this results in multiple challenging behaviours, and this in turn greatly challenges both parents and teachers. It is our belief that to be really respectful of the nature and development of all children as well as their individual particularities and ways of learning, a school curriculum should be carefully designed, carefully taking into account all of the foregoing arguments.

Children should also learn with and through movement – in other words, movement should be integrated into all school subjects, and not be kept as a separate subject or activity, such as Physical Education (PE). Being active in school is important for the child; however, it needs to be a healthy, active movement. Children's natural tendency to learn through movement should be put to positive use. Hopefully, unhealthy movement would then be eradicated, both within themselves and in relation to others.

Some educators have understood the above principles and have developed educational approaches that are more respectful of a child's true nature. Hopefully this welcome trend will continue to develop, for the good of all children. The MISP suggests activities that may help all teachers and children either to cope well within the educational system in which they have to evolve, or to find new, more creative ways to foster learning for children. Experience from around the world is showing that this still comparatively young programme is yielding astonishingly positive benefits both on an individual and on a social level.

"We are quiet after the massage and can concentrate better."

Girl, aged 10

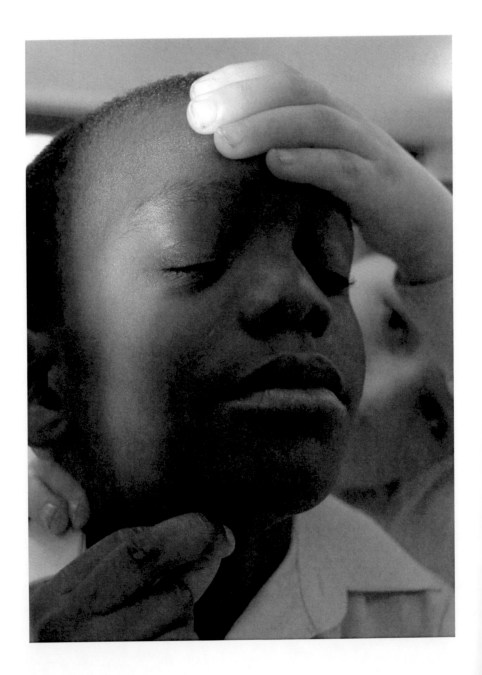

11. Touch and Emotions

Different types of touch can quickly and easily trigger a wide spectrum of emotions. Therefore, we also link touch with emotions. This is easily observed in our everyday language when we talk about people, our relationships, and even ourselves. We can say, "He is such a cold man" or "What a warm personality he has". We can say that we have "tact", that we are "in contact" with another person, or that his words really "touched me". Things can be "touch and go", or you can "touch someone's heart".

At times, touch can be scary and can be used to hurt us. On the other hand, touch can help us to relax, can bring a feeling of love, and be nurturing. Touch is thus "felt" in many different ways. Touch can be aggressive, loving, violent, gentle, painful, tickling, and even magical. There can be all sorts of intentions behind touch: anything is possible, but the intent behind the touch is most assuredly perceived by the person receiving it. Even to say that touch "leaves one cold" is commenting on the effect of touch on our emotional state.

Touch, and the way it is provided, does have physiological effects on/in the body. Both research and new thinking in the philosophy of mind are now breaking down the previously existing Cartesian distinctions between mind, body, and heart. We know that they are interlinked. The body can influence emotions (moods); emotions can influence the body (blushing when we are embarrassed); the body can influence the mind (it's difficult to learn if we are in pain); and the mind can influence the emotions (being nervous when speaking in front of people). A hand on the shoulder can bring comfort and reassurance; holding the hand of a child brings security; a hug can leave us feeling violated but thankfully, more often it leaves us feeling loved.

We also know that children come to school with their own "emotional baggage" being influenced by an almost infinite number of factors. Their own temperaments, their family situation, how they slept, what they ate, if they did not eat, or if something happened on the way to school – these are just a few of the possible factors. The emotional state in which a child enters a classroom can have a drastic effect on her own learning capabilities, on behaviour, and on the relationship with her classmates or the teacher.

A conscious, purposeful, intentional, and positive use of touch with children in both school and home settings can lead to dramatic and positive changes in their behaviour. The many benefits of the MISP have been researched and validated. Ideally, the MISP should be implemented with the highest ethos and professionalism in all schools, and ultimately be regulated and approved globally by all national schooling curricula.

"When my best friend does 'hearts' she always says, 'This is how much I love you'."

Girl, aged 9

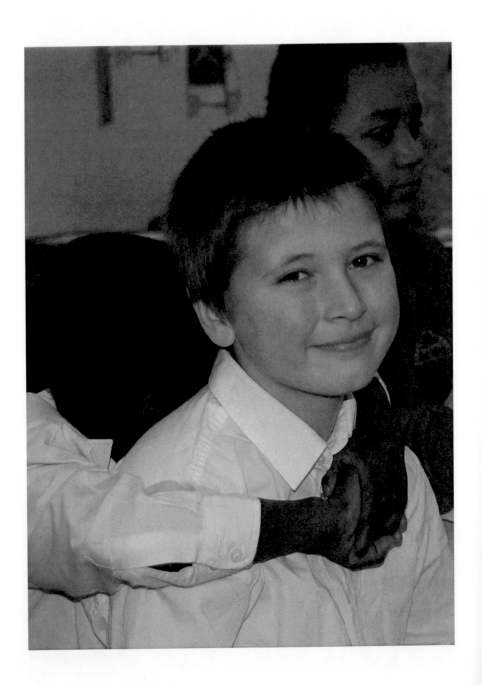

12. Bonding and Attachment

"We can put the child's attachment and sense of trust at risk by imposing adult learning priorities that of necessity are task- rather than child-oriented."

David Elkind

Since the work of the well-known British psychiatrist John Bowlby in the 1950s, hundreds of researchers have been investigating the theories of bonding and attachment. While there is always room for new ideas to emerge about human beings, the idea that a baby and child must have at least one stable "figure of attachment" in order to develop a healthy sense of self has now been widely accepted.

Attachment theories state that a child who has developed a secure attachment will then be able to relate more easily to others. Of course, not all children have that opportunity; however, studies on human resilience are increasingly showing how people can have an extraordinary ability to overcome the greatest of challenges. There are ever more therapeutic approaches based on attachment theory, where the very basic elements of bonding, such as eye contact, and use of voice, smell, touch, rhythm, and respect, are used to help a child's resiliency. In his important book *Bonds of Attachment: Developing Love in Deeply Troubled Children*, Dr Daniel Hughes, an American psychologist, gives us great hope that neglected or abused children can ultimately thrive.

As a child grows, bonds are developed not only with the family, but also with friends, teachers, and classmates. If the initial bonding is lacking, it may result in a child having difficulties in establishing healthy links with her classmates. The MISP incorporates many elements of bonding, the main ones being touch, rhythm, and respect.

Teachers implementing the programme are instructed to be strategic in the pairing of children, which allows them to influence and contribute to a child's ability to develop secure bonds. Strategic pairing can help children to create one-on-one bonds with other children, and improve the collective bonding of the entire class. Instead of connecting with just one or two children, which can lead to cliques and anti-social behaviour, children learn to create bonds with several children. When children in a classroom or even an entire school have the opportunity to experience simple and nurturing contact with all their classmates, a greater sense of security can develop.

"I give my mum massage at home. She says I'm very good and she really likes it."

Girl, aged 7

"Massage makes me behave better."

Boy, aged 10

13. Beyond Guilt and Shame

"Shame is not a warm companion. It turns (her) away from moments of joy as well as feelings of worth and contentment, holding (her) head down and away from the disgusted gazes of (her) parents."

Dr Daniel A Hughes

Since our skin is a crucial "sense organ" used in relating to, and in the discovery of, people and the world around us, the concept of our individual relationship with touch seems worth considering more closely. Each of us has a particular story in regard to touch. That story has been influenced by the culture into which we were born, and in many cases by the touch we received from our primary caregivers.

It is important to understand the fact that our own story with touch may well influence the way we actually perceive touch, and therefore our ideas about the value of massage. Hopefully, this book will convey enough information about the value of touch to encourage a developing enthusiasm for touch and for the Massage In Schools Programme. This chapter calls for more self-reflection, and aims to bring to conscious awareness our emotionally laden views on touch.

Emotions are individual, and it is therefore important to adopt a welcoming attitude toward them. Some people have been touch-deprived, in which case the necessary tools for entering into a relationship that includes nurturing touch may be missing or damaged. These tools can be defined as the capacity to define boundaries for oneself, the capacity to express intimacy via proper sensible touch, and knowing the difference between socially acceptable and unacceptable touch, which is dependent on the degree of intimacy. Touch may simply feel awkward or uncomfortable. Some cultures and families may even have an unofficial minimum-touch policy. This is usually not even a conscious decision, nor is it explicitly acknowledged.

Life may have started with a painful experience, either because of a particularly difficult delivery or possibly because of being born prematurely. There may have been painful, though necessary, medical interventions. Touch may then be connected with pain. This may have even occurred during a time when many people believed that newborn babies did not feel pain. It is true that, up until the 1990s, many hospitals carried out interventions on babies, believing that the baby had not yet developed touch receptors, and thus did not feel pain. However, research has since clearly demonstrated the sensitivity of newborn babies.

Other people may have experienced abuse of different kinds, such as sexual, physical, or emotional abuse. It is very often painful to open our eyes to those realities, regardless of whether they are our own experiences, or the experience of our family, friends, or colleagues. There have been too many years of painful silence about these horrors.

People who survive this type of abuse are often filled with guilt and shame, and an attempt to share their feelings is often a struggle. Fortunately, in the 1990s the collective social denial of abuse began to dissolve, people began to gain the courage to speak the truth about their painful past, and concerted attempts to find solutions began to bloom.

It is never too late to bring healing and to transform painful past experiences and mistakes, both at the individual and the social level. It is possible to move out of guilt and shame in relation to painful events in our lives, and with regards to mistakes we may have committed toward others. Acceptance and forgiveness can find their way into the cells of our body and into the waves of our soul's needs. It may then be possible to consciously participate in re-educating ourselves, and decide to be socially active toward the proper use of touch.

The MISP is a tool for healing the past and for bringing light, thereby creating a brighter and more enlightened future, where nurturing touch will be recognized as essential for human survival and will enable us to truly flourish.

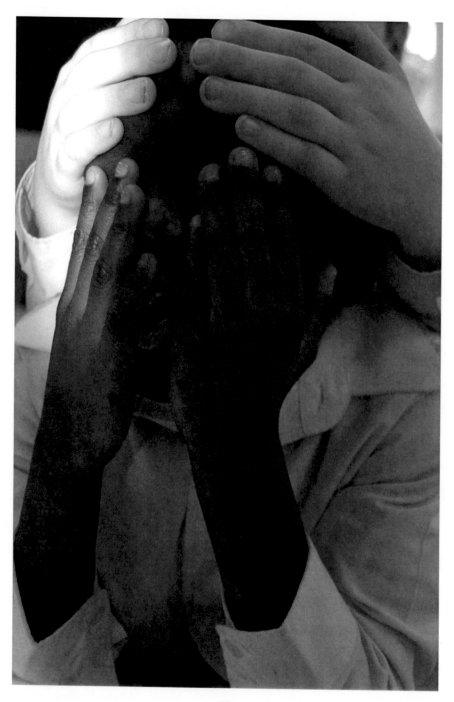

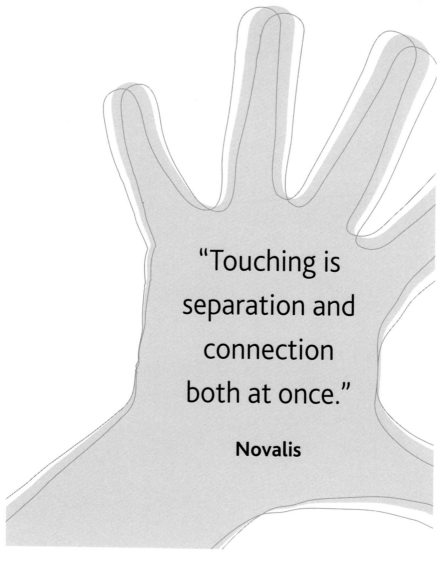

"Touching is
separation and
connection
both at once."

Novalis

14. The Vision

"We all want the best for our children. We want them to be successful at school, accepted and liked by their peers, fair minded and moral. We want them to make good decisions and be kind to others. We want them to have high expectations for their future and have the tools to meet those expectations. Wanting these things is the easy part: equipping our children with the abilities to achieve them is harder."

Karen Reivich and Andrew Shatté

The vision of the MISP is quite simple. All children in all schools should have the opportunity to benefit from nurturing touch every day in every classroom, everywhere in the world. There is no reason, moreover, why this could not become a new global tradition in all cultures across the world.

Researchers have now discovered that human touch is a necessity for healthy human development to occur. Latest research findings in the field of neuroscience support the same conclusion. There exist neither coherent arguments nor any research findings that we are aware of that can cast doubt on the success of the Massage In Schools Programme. Even the fear of paedophilia is not a valid argument against using touch, as it has been shown that most forms of ongoing abuse or neglect result from the *lack* of touch.

When a child goes into another class, or moves to another school, anywhere in the world, the MISP could become a key source of continuity that could bring a sense of security and recognition, as it would be at least one experience with which the child would be familiar.

Our Vision

The vision of the

Massage In Schools Programme

is that every child attending school

experiences positive and

nurturing touch

every day… everywhere

in the world.

15. Origins of the Programme

....

*"If we did not have the use of touch we would all
be totally one. We would dissolve in
the environment as a drop of water in the ocean."*

Albert Soesman

....

The Programme

The idea of bringing positive touch into schools as a programme for children grew naturally from the authors' combined professional skills, our many years of experience, and hours of research and reflection. We concluded that bringing the principle of simple massage, where children would massage one another every day, simply and over clothes, would make a very positive contribution to the lives of children all over the world. A simple non-invasive massage routine was therefore created.

The routine was put together in a flowing movement that also incorporated the development of motor skills. Today, the responsibility for the revision and improvement of the massage routine lies with the Team of International Trainers, a group that includes teachers, massage therapists, nurses, and educators who are qualified to teach the programme.

The massage routine has been very carefully considered from a number of different key perspectives: from those of the health and well-being of the child, from the standpoint of teachers, and from that of schools themselves. We have also taken careful consideration of parents and family life. (A section written especially for parents can be found later in the book – see Chapter 35.) Built into the programme's very design is a comprehensive and holistic approach to child development and the inherent age-appropriate needs at various stages of that development.

The programme, in the form as it is presented in this book, was officially started in the United Kingdom in the year 2000, and it is now expanding globally at an increasingly rapid rate. Whilst touch has, of course, always been present in schools in one form or another, the MISP is the first programme to formally design a recognized, multi-cultural international curriculum respecting children of all cultures. It is therefore the first programme to offer a practical routine that is now taught to Instructors by qualified Trainers, and integrated into schooling systems across many countries and continents.

The Massage In Schools Programme (MISP) gives children a moment to pause and take a breath. Hopefully, it will encourage everyone involved in education to pause, and in the process to re-clarify the deeper meaning of raising, educating, and caring for children. In short, the MISP proposes the universal introduction and embedding of touch and movement into the school curriculum and into school activities more generally. We maintain that movement and touch are necessary for children's healthy learning and well-being ... just as water, air, and food are necessary for their growing bodies.

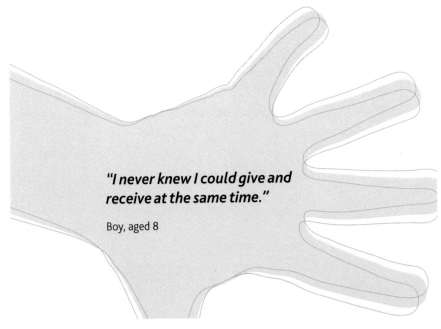

"I never knew I could give and receive at the same time."

Boy, aged 8

"My partner likes it when I do the move called 'ice skating' because I think it makes her soothed and relaxed.

I feel that massage is a very nice thing to do, especially if you're receiving massage and you have done a hard day's work.

Words I use to describe massage are soothing, relaxing, makes you feel sleepy, and soothes your muscles."

Girl, aged 10

16. Has the MISP Been Researched?

*"The evidence, both for animals in general and humans in particular, is unequivocally clear: tactile experience
plays a fundamentally important role in the growth and development of all mammals thus far studied...."*

Ashley Montagu

Numerous studies and research projects on touch and massage have been carried out from many angles and perspectives all over the world. The results of these studies unambiguously point to the essential importance of touch, and the many positive effects that massage holds for people of all ages, from premature babies to the elderly. When the MISP was first introduced to the United Kingdom in 2000, no official studies had been carried out on the programme. Since then, however, there have been a number of studies and research projects conducted (see website: *www.massageinschools.com*). The studies and research, together with strong anecdotal evidence and recorded observations by teachers, all strongly attest to the way in which massage has made significant positive changes in pupils' emotional well-being and constructive social behaviour. Further studies and research projects are currently under way, the results of which will be made available by those responsible for our programme development on the website.

Reputable research into the value of, and the benefits arising from, massage for the physical, emotional, and mental dimensions of human experience has now convinced even the sceptics. Research on this specific programme is beginning to mushroom, and clearly demonstrates its positive effects, indexed by key variables such as the reduction of violence in schools, lower noise levels in classrooms, a diminution of bullying on school premises, and an improvement in children's concentration levels.

17. Key Characteristics of the Programme

"...research points out that having one good friend
is enough to restore self-esteem and
social acceptance, especially if
the friendship is 'validating and caring'."

Elaine N. Aron

Inclusivity

The MISP is for all children of all cultures and religious beliefs. When practised in the classroom, all children can be involved. Some situations may require flexibility; for example, culture and/or religion may dictate that genders may not be crossed, in which case only girls can work with girls and boys with boys. Regardless of the situation, each child is to be included.

Peer massage

Only children massage each other. Neither school teachers nor the MISP Instructor massage the children, nor do they demonstrate the routine on them.

Easy and accessible

The programme's routine can easily be learned in a few days by all the children, under the direction of the MISP Instructor. There are very few materials needed.

Freedom of choice

Children always ask, and are asked for their permission, before the massage routine begins. The child has the right to say "yes" or "no" to massage. This shows the children that they are respected, as well as encouraging them to respect their classmates.

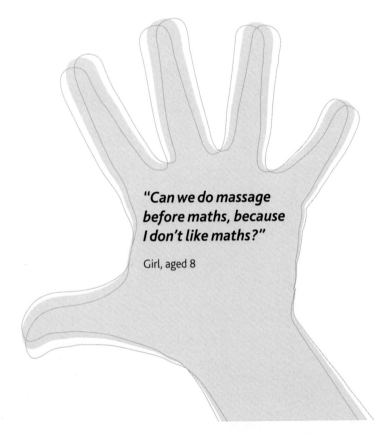

"Can we do massage before maths, because I don't like maths?"

Girl, aged 8

"I do 'shampoo' on mummy when I come home. She loves it."

Girl, aged 4

"To feel with another is to care."

Daniel Goleman

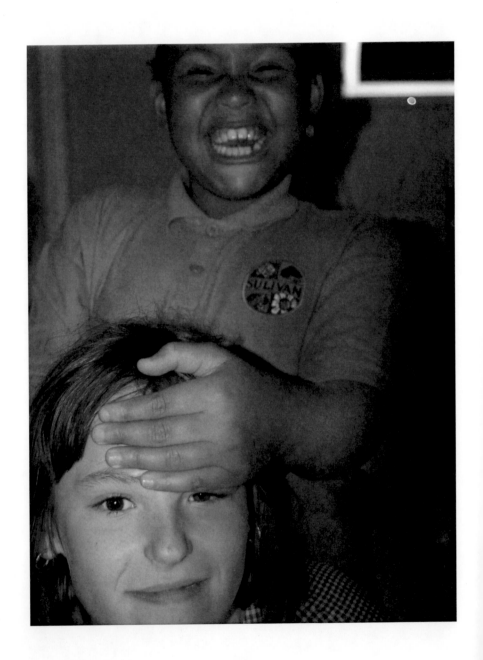

18. Can Something This Good Be Healthy?

"Socially connected people are less prone to stress.
Social support seems to keep increased heart rate,
blood pressure and stress hormones from running amok."

Dr Aric Sigman

Benefits of the MISP for children

As research study results on the MISP become available, and as teachers share their observations, the list of benefits for children continues to increase. Teachers are encouraged to try the programme, and to draw their own conclusions from their own direct experience. Teachers can also keep simple observation charts and data concerning various aspects of the programme that might need attention.

From these charts, as well as from documented observations, a broad consensus is emerging on the list of discernible benefits. Listed below are the main benefits that have been observed within classrooms and schools.

1. Reduction in stress levels

Nurturing touch and massage reduce stress levels. This has been measured bio-chemically in our bodies. Constant high stress levels may lead to a range of behavioural problems, such as impatience, violent behaviour, sleep disturbance, hyperactivity, and a weak immune system. Children in modern society are often over-stimulated or, paradoxically, deprived and under-stimulated. Massage regulates their stress levels, introducing much-needed balance and thus helping to reduce the aforementioned consequences.

2. Higher self-esteem

Authentic touch enhances the sense of self, which is in turn crucial to finding our unique place in society. When children are lovingly touched, their sense of well-being is enhanced, and they feel important, cared for, seen, and loved, which are all building blocks for enhanced self-esteem.

Because the MISP is for all children, without discrimination, a sense of equality emerges where there is no competition. There are no good or bad marks with massage, no first or last places. The feedback emerges naturally and spontaneously from our massage partner.

3. Emotional competency/intelligence

Because ultimately every child ends up massaging and being massaged by every other child, they all experience the richest of learning environments – learning, for example, about adjusting, respecting, difference(s), empathy, sensitivity, boundaries, self-awareness, and so on. Moreover, all this occurs quite unconsciously when the MISP becomes a regular routine in the child's day.

4. Literacy/vocabulary

Learning the MISP naturally increases children's vocabulary at many levels. Physically, they can learn body parts and the names of muscles. They learn how to describe their preferences in regard to the massage routine and how firm or slowly they like the massage. Numerous touch activities can be carried out in relation to language, fostering the learning and integration processes for many children.

5. Improved concentration/attention

It has been observed many times that children who experience regular massage are able to concentrate for longer periods of time. Their attention is more acute, which is probably related to the reduction of stress levels combined with a sense of well-being. As adults, when we are over-stressed it is far more difficult for us to concentrate, and this is true for children too. Today, many children have stressful lives, and the MISP can help to alleviate at least some of this stress.

6. Integrated knowledge

Schooling systems are beginning to appreciate the fact that children tend to be more kinaesthetic learners than anything else, even if each child is unique and also manifests individualized ways of learning. The way many schooling systems deal with intellectual learning puts a great deal of pressure on many children, especially younger children, as this is not their main way of learning.

The unfolding of intellectual learning for children from 4 to 12 years of age is a very subtle process, and progressive holistic educators such as Drs Maria Montessori and Rudolf Steiner have emphasized the importance of never forcing this process. They claim that learning should always be linked with the sense of play, and with activities that involve the body as well as the faculty of imagination. This has been clearly demonstrated and supported by recent neuroscientific research. Children will gain optimum brain unfolding and balanced bodily neurobiological activity if their whole being is solicited in their learning process.

Research is now showing that many children struggle with the "over-intellectualization" of schooling, which puts too much emphasis on "head" activities. With the MISP and the ideas of touch and movement incorporated into school subjects, the organic, natural learning and integration of school subjects is promoted in a way that acknowledges and respects the true nature of children.

7. Positive experiences of touch

Too many children have had negative experiences with touch, or else a very limited experience of touch. Although the skin is actually our body's largest organ, positive touch often tends to be neglected. The MISP can thus provide an opportunity for children to learn about nurturing touch in a non-threatening way, establishing a positive foundation for the rest of their lives.

8. Learning about giving and receiving

The programme is designed so that all children have the opportunity to both give and receive massage. It is healthy for the children to alternate these roles equally, at both a conscious and an unconscious level. It helps them to develop the essential social abilities involved in both receiving and giving.

9. Social competency

Children will learn about differences by simply touching their peers in a positive way. They will learn to be flexible within the context of this approach to touch. Strategic planning will ensure that all the children in a classroom will end up massaging all the other children at some point; thus, each child establishes links with all of their classmates.

10. A healthy way of learning about love and intimacy

Studies and research projects have shown that children who have experienced nurturing touch have a solid foundation for experiencing intimacy, and have a better chance of establishing successful adult relationships. With this programme, children work one-on-one, thus developing empathy for and sensitivity toward one another. On an individual basis, both of these are necessary prerequisites for healthy relationships.

11. A new way of communicating with their parents

Many children bring MISP back to their homes after school. This becomes a new way of communicating with their parents; and because of the effects of nurturing touch, the child may well begin to experience a more loving relationship with their parents.

It has been reported by parents in school meetings that the children who experience massage in school begin to do the massage on their parents, as well as seeming to get on better with their siblings. Children thus benefit from a new type of contact with their parents, who may also benefit by a reduction in their own stress levels. There are many possible secondary spin-off benefits that can be derived from the programme – this is just one of many examples.

12. A right to say "yes" or "no" to touch

Asking permission before massaging is a mandatory part of the MISP. In many situations, the MISP is one of the few times that children truly experience having choices about touch.

It is sad but true that children's integrity is often invaded by disturbing touch. An adult's intention is generally pure; however the child can experience touch as invasive. The touch can be a medical intervention or an unwanted hug from a family member or friend. In some cases the touch is actually abusive, both physically and/or psychologically.

When permission is sought before the massage, or before any touch activity linked with the school curriculum, the child starts to understand the meaning of respect (both self-respect and respect for others) and therefore develops a greater sense of identity and self-worth.

19. Making the Teacher's Life Easier

"The aim of the regular school is no less than to help children and adolescents become human beings in the best sense of the word. It has to educate the child to become a human being."

Coenraad van Houten

The benefits of massage to children are numerous and far-reaching, but there are significant benefits for the teacher as well.

A new tool

Many teachers struggle, being challenged on the one hand by a compulsory and sometimes inflexible state curriculum about which they have little if any say, and on the other hand by children's behaviour which has become more and more demanding. While this programme should never be treated as a utilitarian tool for making children comply with an educational system, it is found that when teachers start the day with massage in their classrooms, they discover that they have a twofold tool.

First, they have a tool that benefits them because of the benefits it has on the children in their classroom; and secondly, it provides a means of fostering creativity. If teachers dare to bring movement and touch into their day-to-day methodologies, they may well regain and/or experience an increased joy in teaching, allowing their own imagination and creative skills to flourish.

A calmer class

The effects of massage on children simply provide a more manageable class for the teacher. Studies and research projects have shown that the MISP can justifiably be regarded as an effective means of class management because of its calming effects, and because it heightens social skills between the children.

New status among children

Teachers who have implemented the programme in their classrooms have gained a renewed popularity amongst their pupils. This helps to balance out what many teachers experience as a challenge: being the one who imposes unwanted work. Bringing the MISP into the classroom is also highly innovative – and children commonly appreciate innovations.

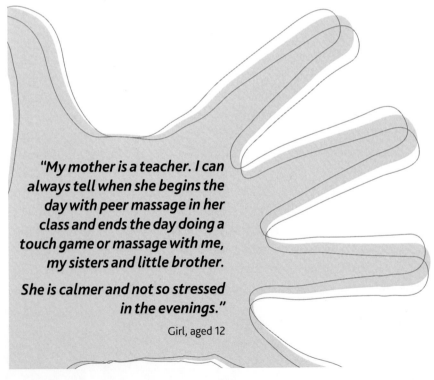

"My mother is a teacher. I can always tell when she begins the day with peer massage in her class and ends the day doing a touch game or massage with me, my sisters and little brother.

She is calmer and not so stressed in the evenings."

Girl, aged 12

20. Comments and Observations from Teachers

"An understanding heart is everything in a teacher, and cannot be esteemed highly enough. One looks back with appreciation to the brilliant teachers, but with gratitude to those who touched our human feeling. The curriculum is so much necessary raw material, but warmth is the vital element for the growing plant and for the soul of the child. "

Carl Jung

"The first thing I noticed when children came into my classroom and already knew the massage, is that they were more respectful to their classmates and to me."

"I've noticed changes in how the children show consideration, and share and resolve conflicts."

"The children in my class now ask permission to play with a toy or borrow a pencil. Before the massage, they usually took it, without asking."

"Children are more willing to sit next to each other. They relate better to each other."

"After the morning massage, I can actually do my job, and teach!"

"Class members are more compassionate."

"When we do massage, everyone immediately calms."

"They will happily participate with everyone now when we do massage. At first they only wanted to massage their particular friends."

"When we started, one child was rigid, unsure, and unable to relate to other class members. Now he is more flexible and more talkative in class."

"Massage really calms down the boys in my class."

"I'm sure of its effectiveness for art activities. I've used it a lot, particularly before observational drawings."

"The massage really did establish a sense of communication in my class, something I wanted but was not able to get otherwise."

"It's great at lunchtime; in the dinner queue they all give each other a massage."

"I have noticed that the relationships between children in the schoolyard have greatly improved since beginning massage. Children are now asked to join in games, and we rarely find a child left playing alone."

"In my class, I have decided to do the massage both in the morning before school begins, and after lunch. I noticed a difference within a matter of days."

"Children need a routine, and doing this for a few minutes every morning before we start our day works well in my classroom."

"An OFSTED (Office for Standards in Education) Inspector said: 'This is a very good lesson with some outstanding features… excellent responses from children, high levels of learning and achievement. The level of maturity displayed by these young children is amazing!'"

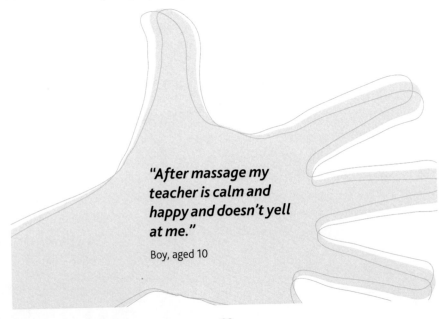

"After massage my teacher is calm and happy and doesn't yell at me."

Boy, aged 10

"This is the best thing I ever done in school."

Boy, aged 9

21. One for All and All for One...

"Improving our ability to converse means improving our ability to interact socially."

Heinz Zimmermann

The entire classroom benefits from the MISP in many ways. Here are some of the observed benefits.

Increased knowledge of one another

The fact that children usually end up massaging all of their classmates leads to more knowledge of one another and, normally, greater sociability.

Reduction of cliques

The MISP also assists in decreasing the frequency of sub-group formation, and the prevalence of cliques. These groups are often challenging for some children, as well as for the teacher to manage.

Decrease in anti-social behaviour

It has been observed that even students who have been the worst of enemies in the classroom begin to show respect for each other. Even if they are not paired up with each other until later on, it is nearly impossible to be harsh with someone whom you have just massaged, or from whom you have received a massage. Therefore, there is less anti-social behaviour.

Decrease in bullying

The main causes of bullying seem to include a lack of positive touch experiences, low self-esteem, and negative peer influences. The MISP helps to transform many of these influences, thus helping to reduce the incidence of bullying.

Lower noise level in the classroom

A study carried out in Sweden in 2003 found that noise level significantly decreased in the classroom following the introduction of the MISP. Not only was the noise level significantly reduced during the study itself, but the effect persisted after the study was complete. The children continued to massage each other, and the teachers later reported that the noise level continued to be much lower compared to the situation before the implementation of the MISP.

Group bonding, and bonding between individuals

Social circles help to secure attachments, and are among the basic elements that help each child to develop to their fullest potential. Because of how it works in the classroom, the MISP is one of the greatest tools for effecting loving bonds amongst children.

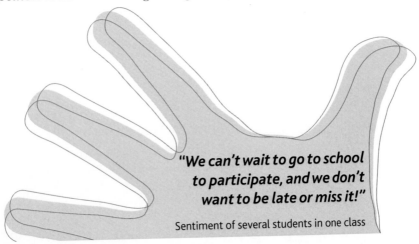

"We can't wait to go to school to participate, and we don't want to be late or miss it!"

Sentiment of several students in one class

22. Benefits of the MISP for the Entire School

"In a cut-throat world, school is a battle ground where the only thing that matters is coming top of the class."

Carl Honoré

The entire school benefits from the MISP. When the programme has been implemented, the following benefits have been observed.

- less violence in the classroom and on the school grounds
- more games and activities amongst the children
- less graffiti
- children caring more for the appearance of their school
- higher attendance levels
- less exclusions
- children come to school on time so as not to miss out on the massage
- teachers are healthier and have less sick days
- effective, inspirational meetings

Touch activities can be used in staff meetings to begin or end the meeting, thereby lightening, inspiring, and making these meetings more effective.

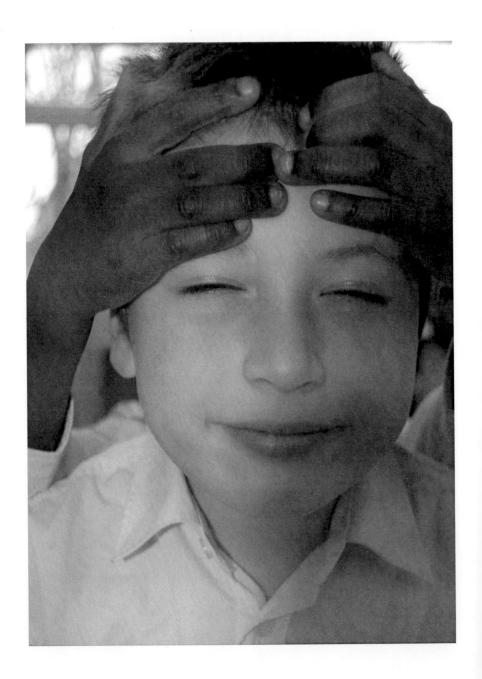

23. Can It Get any Better than This?

*"We have to imagine and practice a life that can make life
on earth in the coming decades and centuries possible:
a way of being that can give younger generations
— those who are entrusted to our care —
the trust and confidence that human existence
on earth is worthwhile and precious,
that it has meaning and sense."*

Friedemann Schwarzkopf

Benefits of the MISP for society as a whole

As the Massage In Schools Programme continues to spread around the world, it is important to keep alive the long-term vision with everyone who works with the programme; for it is ideals and vision that stimulate the will to put things into practice and bring them to fruition.

It is surely not too grandiose to suggest that we can begin to visualize a better society, in light of the previously mentioned manifold benefits. Such global benefits could, at the very least, include:

- more respect
- reduced violence
- reduced abuse (at all levels)
- a healthier population
- reduction in health costs
- reductions in drug and alcohol abuse
- less crime

- a more loving society
- a more peaceful world to live in

Of course, there is no way to tell in advance, or with any degree of accuracy, just how massage could affect the future. However, those who work with the MISP believe in evolution and the enhancement of the human condition, and we firmly believe that this programme can become one of the major contributions to the well-being of humanity. While it begins with our children, it has benefits for us all, both today and in the future.

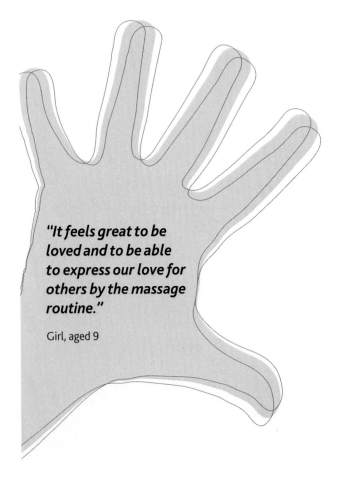

"It feels great to be loved and to be able to express our love for others by the massage routine."

Girl, aged 9

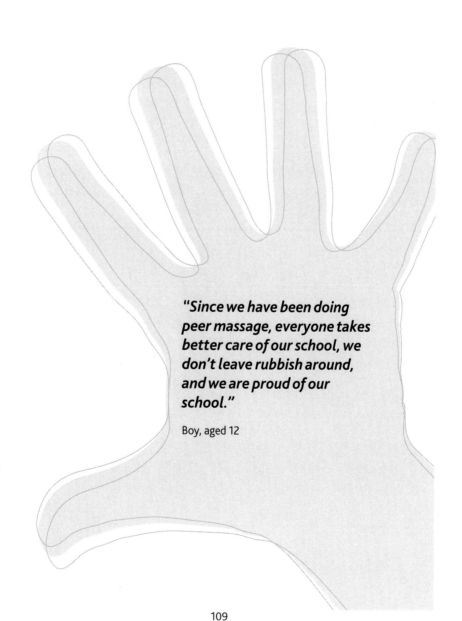

"Since we have been doing peer massage, everyone takes better care of our school, we don't leave rubbish around, and we are proud of our school."

Boy, aged 12

Les lunettes

La cuillère

Mas

Eye glasses

ing

24. Observations and Research/Studies

*"Research, overall, strongly suggests that fast pace
and special effects can interfere with
development of active learning habits."*

Jane M. Healy

Although more and more research and studies are being conducted on the MISP, and with excellent results, teachers are strongly encouraged to draw their own conclusions about the programme, based on their own direct experience of its diverse benefits. Studies and research projects are, in essence, documented observations and organized information. Many aspects related to the MISP can be observed, qualified, and quantified. Teachers are generally very busy, so the idea of collecting data may appear daunting and overwhelming. However, becoming aware of the effects of the programme creates a self-generating momentum which helps to sustain it, encouraging the sharing of information about it with others, including informing parents and colleagues – all contributing to an atmosphere of confidence in the value of the programme.

Teachers are encouraged to choose what they would like to observe, and to create their own observation sheets. If help is needed, any MISP Instructor coming into the classroom has knowledge of how to conduct observations appropriately, and would be more than willing to assist the teacher in implementing a small study in their own classroom.

Below are some ideas of what variables can be observed:

- one child's behaviour
- any change of behaviour of the entire class

- social interactions
- class atmosphere
- types of physical contact
- language
- levels of noise in the classroom
- attention span
- cliques and sub-group evolution
- incidence of bullying

Teachers are encouraged to begin to conduct the observations before the MISP is implemented, and then at short intervals afterwards, as it is all too easy to forget, or recall inaccurately, the typical behaviour of the children before the programme was implemented.

"Massage helps us relax, learn, think, breathe, and not get distracted, and calms us down."

Boy, aged 9

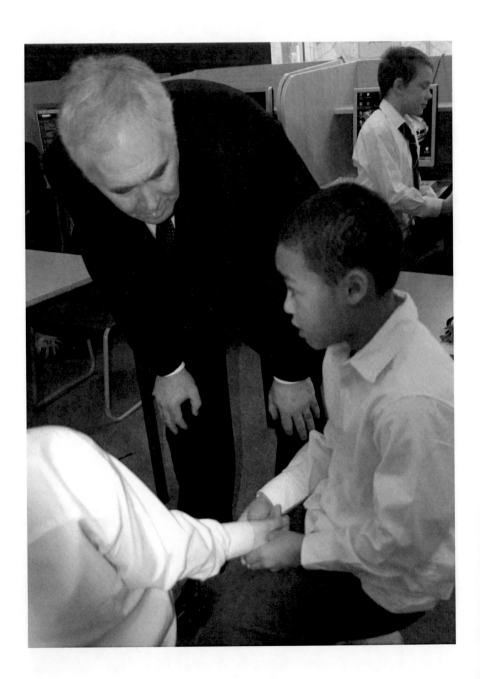

25. Child Protection

"Many of the scientific discoveries in the field of emotion look like reinventing the wheel. They affirm the importance of touch, of responsiveness, of giving time to people. How can we legislate for these things?"

Sue Gerhardt

All legal requirements must be followed

Requirements for child protection will vary from country to country, from town to town, and sometimes from school to school. Therefore, it is mandatory for Instructors to get information about all child-protection laws, requirements, and policies that are in effect, before implementing MISP in any school or institution. Each teacher bringing the MISP into the classroom must also be aware of the applicable child-protection policies.

Fear

Many adults are sceptical about any new programme, including one introducing nurturing touch. Fear of abuse and/or paedophilia may be the origin of many doubts and fears. Cultural interpretation surrounding touch may also bring different reactions. We face a paradox here. It is our belief that one of the causes of abuse toward children is a lack of proper, nurturing touch right from birth, within the educational system, and in society in general. Therefore, part of the solution to counteracting abuse lies in the promotion of nurturing touch, both in family life and within the educational system. However, it is important to understand that as soon as we deal with nurturing touch, reactions are possible. You may observe reactions from your colleagues, teachers, and parents, and sometimes unexpected reactions from the children. There are several different ways of reducing doubt, fear, scepticism, or resistance to touch. Two main aspects need to be considered regarding child protection for the MISP Instructors.

Proper information

The first aspect is proper information, which includes the MISP itself – what it is, and how it works. It is especially important to mention: that children massage each other; that they give massage only after asking and receiving permission; and that the child has the right to say "yes" or "no" to the massage. Information on studies done on massage can help to bring peace of mind regarding the MISP.

Reactions from children will be multiple, of course. An important issue is that some children might be experiencing nurturing touch for the first time. It may be the first time someone has asked their permission, or that they have been given the right to say "no". They will start to experience touch as something acceptable, and it may trigger something deep inside them. They may have been confronted with other types of realities regarding touch, and it may have been painful. It may bring confusion about what touch really is. Finally, it may bring them to talk to the teacher or the Instructor about what they have previously experienced with touch. This may be expressed by words such as: "I know an adult who touches me without first asking my permission." The teacher or the Instructor must then follow the guidelines outlined under the child-protection policy of that school.

Under the auspices of the MISP, Instructors and teachers should avoid talking too intimately to the child about potential abuse, as this would go beyond their role. Of course, Instructors and teachers always welcome a child's sharing, but they must be careful to avoid making a promise to a child that their "secret" will be kept. This can place the

Instructor or the teacher in a delicate position, as the trust of the child may be at stake.

Courage and honesty are required. If the child starts by saying, "I have a secret", the Instructor and the teacher need to have the courage to explain to the child that they may need to share the secret with someone who can help them be safe. It is important to understand that the MISP was not founded with the goal of discovering when children are abused; but the very nature of the programme may, of course, lead to such discoveries.

We may not know what these children have experienced. Keep in mind that we are not responsible for what has happened to them, and unless we are qualified and educated in this field, we should not judge the situation, nor try to repair it. Yet because we are responsible, caring adults, we have a moral and legal responsibility toward the children. This brings us to the second aspect of child protection.

Responsibility to take action

As mentioned at the beginning of this chapter, before implementing the MISP in a school, in a classroom, or within any community, all Instructors must know about the relevant establishment's legal aspects and policies for child protection. These policies and procedures must be respected and must be complied with whenever any doubts arise about what a child might be expressing in relation to abuse. Any doubts that we may have concerning a child need to be reported to the proper authorities.

The matter is being raised here in order to inform readers that all MISP Trainers and Instructors are well prepared to follow the child-protection policies of the country in which they live or the school with which they work.

"Whatever you can do,

or dream you can, begin it.

Boldness has genius,

power, and magic in it."

Goethe

26. What is the Programme?

"For the first time in human history, most of the stories are told to most of the children not by their parents, their school, or their church, but by a group of distant corporations that have something to sell."

George Gerbner

There are three main aspects in this programme. The first is the actual Massage In Schools Programme Routine itself. The second is the incorporation of touch and movement into the school's national curriculum subjects; and the third one comprises activities that involve touch and movement. All of these are covered in the intensive Massage in Schools Programme Instructors Course.

1.   The Massage In Schools Programme Routine

This consists of several massage movements that children do on each other, one-on-one. The children are seated at their desks or sitting on mats placed on the floor, and the massage is carried out over their clothes, on the back, arms, and head. It is most beneficial if the routine is done every morning before school begins. The full routine takes approximately 7–8 minutes, in other words, about 15 minutes in total for both children to massage each other.

Instructors are taught the full routine in the Massage In Schools Programme Instructors Course, and they are then qualified to teach the routine to children by demonstrating the massage on another adult or in the air.

2.   Touch Games and Activities

These are simple activities that can be carried out at any time, at the convenience or discretion of the teacher, thereby bringing touch and movement into the normal school day. They can be used for a variety of reasons, such as developing social skills, creating a break to improve their ability to concentrate, or just for a bit of fun. Some suggestions for touch games and activities are included in the latter part of the book.

3.   Touch and Movement into the School Curriculum Subjects

Teachers are encouraged to incorporate touch and movement as a significant aspect of their teaching methodology in the delivery of national or core curriculum subjects. All subjects can be taught with touch and movement. There are general ideas for some subjects given at the end of the book.

All three aspects of the MISP can be applied at home with the child, and indeed with all members of their family.

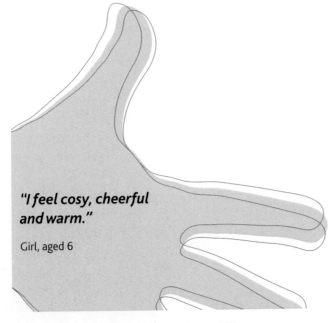

"I feel cosy, cheerful and warm."

Girl, aged 6

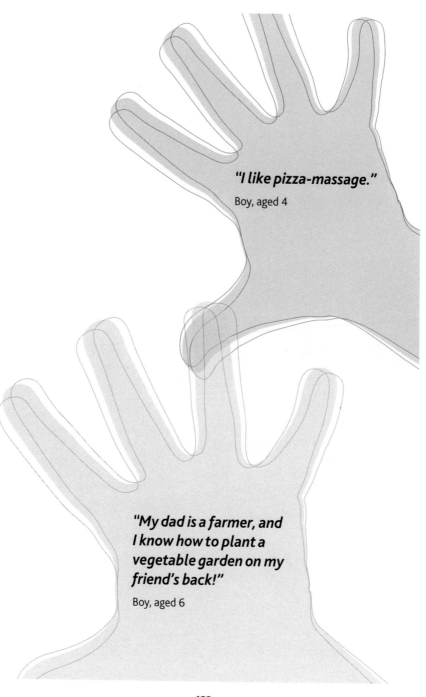

"*I like pizza-massage.*"

Boy, aged 4

"*My dad is a farmer, and I know how to plant a vegetable garden on my friend's back!*"

Boy, aged 6

27. The Massage In Schools Programme Routine

"The responsibility of educators is to create oases for children."

René Quérido

The MISP Routine is only taught on MISP Instructors Courses. While the routine is easy to implement in the classroom, it is important that it is taught properly, and that both the routine and, especially, the children are respected.

The programme is simple. Behind the procedural simplicity, however, lies a great deal of thought, effort, and expertise that have been put into the development of the programme. It works because dedicated Instructors make it look easy for the teachers and children to do. Furthermore, respect is always held paramount for everyone involved in the process.

The programme is primarily experiential in nature, and as a result it cannot be learned and understood adequately through the printed word alone. Moreover, physical touch can occasionally cause previously unprocessed issues of abuse to rise to the surface. Therefore, a fully participative training in the delivery of the programme becomes especially important. In order to protect the quality and integrity of the programme, the actual routine will not be reproduced in this book. However, if teachers, parents, governors, or head teachers would like to begin to introduce related activities into the classroom, there are several touch games and movements, which are described later. As mentioned earlier, please remember that asking permission of and thanking the recipient, which are integral parts of the programme, should also be included in any touch games that are used.

Information about your closest Massage In Schools Association (MISA) Branch, MISP Trainer, and MISP Instructor, along with the list of all MISP Trainings internationally, can be found on the website at:

www.massageinschools.com

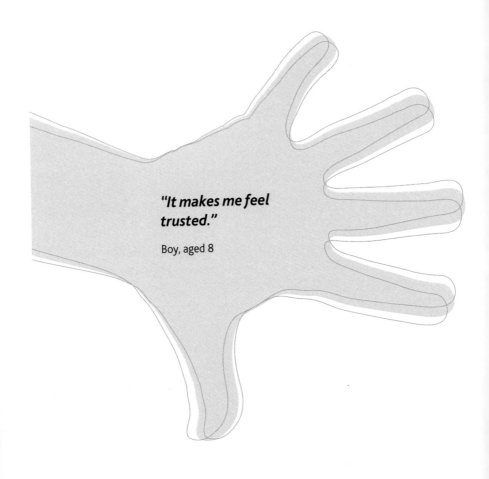

"It makes me feel trusted."

Boy, aged 8

"It made me feel safe."

Girl, aged 11

28. How Does It Work?

"...a child's attachment behaviour is activated especially by pain, fatigue, and anything frightening."

John Bowlby

In order to implement the programme, teachers, parents, school staff members, and others need to take a two-day course to learn more about the MISP. The other option is that the school engages the services of an already trained MISP Instructor to teach the routine to the children of the class.

While some may be tempted to try to implement the programme directly from this book, it is strongly advised that teachers either take the course themselves, or find someone who is already trained and who can support the learning of the routine, and implement it successfully. It is important that the quality of the programme be maintained and that the high reputation and credibility of MISP are kept intact.

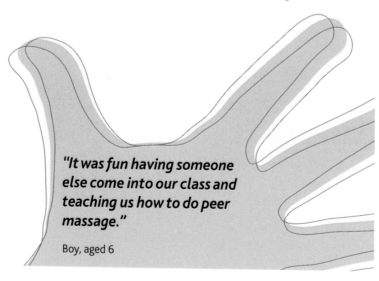

"It was fun having someone else come into our class and teaching us how to do peer massage."

Boy, aged 6

29. When to Use the Routine

"Bumper stickers that ask, 'Have you hugged your child today?' are disappearing as parents become wary of touching their own children. This behaviour, reminiscent of an earlier, more formal time, is not a good idea, because children need touch for survival. Their growth and development thrive on touch. And how will they learn about love and affection if not through touch?"

Tiffany Field

From the studies and research projects that have been carried out by those working with the MISP, it appears that the best time to do the massage routine is first thing in the morning. Research has discovered a noticeable change in punctuality – with children coming to school on time more often in order to enjoy the massage: they just don't want to miss it! It has also helped the children to begin their school day in a positive way, even if their morning at home started out negatively. Teachers have found that if they begin the massage first thing in the morning, they can then go directly into teaching a classroom full of children who are settled and ready to concentrate and learn.

Of course, it is up to the teacher to decide when and how they feel the routine fits best into their teaching schedule. Some teachers have also carried out the routine directly after lunch, or else after break. A few teachers have even offered the routine both first thing in the morning and directly after lunch. Some teachers even do the routine again at the end of the day for a smooth transition between school and home.

30. The Importance of Rhythm

"You direct the impulse of will not by telling him what is right, but by letting him experience rhythm day after day."

Rudolf Steiner

Rhythm is part of the universe. The word "universe" can even be defined as one song (uni + verse). Rhythm is part of life and is part of our body. Our hearts beat rhythmically, we breathe rhythmically, and we move rhythmically. Our days are filled with rhythm, such as our sleep patterns and our daily meals. There is also rhythm in our weekly routines. Rhythm is found in the passing of seasons and the months of the year, in the movement of the moon, and the ebb and flow of the tides. Rhythm gives all of us a sense of security and a foundation on which to stand. For children, rhythm is of crucial importance, and should be given prime consideration within education.

Education needs a rhythm. Visualize construction: there is a rhythm when building a physical foundation with physical building blocks. In the same way, education is built on building blocks. Rhythm and repetition have an impact on the integration and the forming of children. It is therefore recommended that a discernible rhythm be created for the massage routine in the classroom, and that it is made to come alive for the children. A daily routine at the same time is the best kind of rhythm. If the teacher decides not to do it every day, then there should still be a rhythm – for example, every Monday, Wednesday, and Friday, or perhaps once a week at the same time on the same day.

There are also various simple touch activities that can be adopted by teachers and/or parents, which can become part of the school and/or family rhythmic routine.

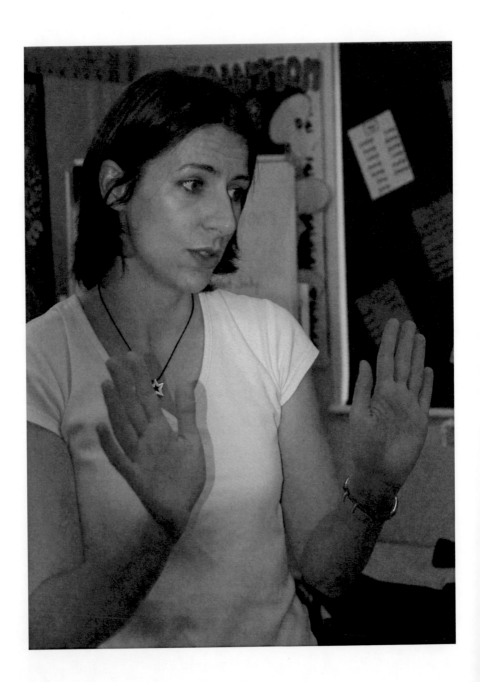

31. Implementation of the Routine

"When stress piles upon stress without the relief of an equal portion of relaxation, the body begins to shut out all sensory intake and the learning process is completely blocked."

Vimala McClure

Various factors need to be considered in the implementation of the MISP. These include: ages of the children, number of children, parental approval, pairing of children, and training.

1. Training/practising

If you wish to become familiar with the strokes it is suggested that you invite an Instructor to come to your class/school. If you are interested in becoming an official Instructor, you must take the two-day course yourself to gain a full understanding of the programme and to master the massage routine.

2. Informing colleagues and parents

The adults in the child's immediate life must be fully informed about the programme: the head teacher, other teachers, and above all the parents. Everyone must of course follow school policies concerning parents' permission regarding new activities. Emphasizing that only children massage each other, and that adults never massage the children under any circumstances, can be very reassuring to anyone with concerns. They should also be informed of the fact that each child will be asked permission before any massage is started, and the child has the right to say "yes" or "no". It might be hard for a child to say "no" when virtually all the other children say "yes!" with enthusiasm. Therefore, teachers are trained to be aware of and recognize this issue, and make sure that no stigma whatsoever is attached to saying "no".

3. Preparing the children

Once parents and the school authorities have agreed, children need to be informed beforehand that the programme will be introduced. Showing them photographs or a video may be appropriate and helpful.

4. Environment

The atmosphere and ambience created for the MISP routine need to be given a great deal of attention. Additionally, regardless of the choice of environment, it is important that it always stays the same.

In creating an ambience, teachers choose what feels appropriate for them, and for their classroom and children. Blinds can be closed in order to create a certain effect or a sense of containment. Dimming lights may help the children to calm down and relax. The teacher decides what is needed for the routine:

- how the children are to be placed
- whether the desks are to be moved or if the chairs are to be placed in a circle. (Note: a rhythm should be established in the moving of desks and chairs. In other words, they should be moved the same way each time.)
- whether the children are to remain seated at their own desks
- whether the children are to sit on the floor. (Exercise mats are perfect for this purpose, and are light and easy to store, or small pieces/samples of carpeting can also be used.)
- whether candles should be lit or essential oils be burned. (Some

teachers have experimented with essential oil burners. The children have then associated the smell with the routine. If oil is used, we suggest mandarin oil, as this has been recognized as the only oil that has a balancing effect on children.)

- how the process of washing and wiping their hands is to be implemented. (Having wipes beside the children's desks is encouraged.)

No matter what the choice of environment, it is crucial that, once established, it stays the same. We can easily destabilize the children if we frequently change the environment or the way they move in it. By keeping the environment and the routine the same, the children move into the rhythm of it. As a result, their entire being flows into and through the activity and an inner security is successfully established.

5. Pairing the children

Children work one-on-one with the MISP routine. Especially in the beginning, the pairing process needs to be carefully considered by the teacher in order to create as successful an implementation as possible. When there is an uneven number of children, one child can become the teacher's assistant and do the routine "in the air" for the other children.

The teacher will need to be strategic, and to be the one to choose who works with whom. We usually find that pairing children who get along well together is the best initial strategy. As always, social dynamics will be in play amongst the children. It is crucial for the teacher to retain responsibility for pairing children together, since inclusion as well as the empowerment of children is paramount within the programme. The teacher will be able to strategically choose to pair the children who are less in contact with one another, once all children are familiar with the routine.

Once the routine has become second nature for the children and part of their day-to-day life in school, the opportunity to pair the children randomly opens up, for example, by drawing names, or by pairing them based on hair colour.

6. Time duration for implementing

This will depend upon multiple factors, such as:

- age of children
- how children respond/learn
- the time at which the teacher wishes to offer the routine
- the availability of the MISP Instructor if the programme is implemented in this way

There are 15 strokes to be learned, and it is our experience that children aged 4–6 can learn approximately three per session. With children 7–9 years old, you can increase the number to four or five per session. Older children can certainly learn seven or eight strokes per session. These are, of course, just averages. The individual strokes are repeated several times so that the children can integrate the strokes. In addition, the strokes that the child learned previously should be repeated at each learning session.

"Miss, can we put massage on the timetable?"

Girl, aged 7

"Teacher, teacher, when is our massage time today?"

Girl, aged 9

32. Touch, Movement, and School Subjects

*"Learning is not just about reading, writing,
and maths…Learning begins in space…
The years of optimum right-hemisphere development
are years when learning is still strongly linked to
sensory-motor activity."*

Sally Goddard Blythe

Research and the observation of children have shown that children from 4 to 12 years of age are primarily kinaesthetic learners. This means that their entire body needs to be involved in the learning process. Although this is generally known, we find that most school systems seem to forget or omit to put it into practice. Of course, movement happens at breaks and in gym or PE lessons, but movement seems to be compartmentalized and separated from the learning that takes place in the classroom. In the classroom, children are reminded to sit still. However, children hear more if their body is actively involved: the MISP ethos is to "live the knowledge", and seamlessly bring touch and movement into curriculum subjects.

With a little imagination, many ideas can be found that effectively introduce touch and movement into the various subjects. On the next page are some ideas for various subjects as well as age groups; and on the pages following the chart, you will find clearer explanations of how the activities can be carried out.

Chart of Touch Games

Subjects	Age 4–6	Age 7–9	Age 10–12
Geography	Do weather massage, see Touch Games	Draw landscapes on backs	Draw shapes of countries on backs
History	Act out characters of local legends	Draw pictures of country's flag/emblem	Create a mummy
Languages	Draw images on backs	Learn the alphabet	Learn words in foreign languages
Maths	Write simple numbers on backs	Do times tables with balls	Find geometric forms with their peers
Music	Clap in rhythm	Sing songs that involve touch	Move hands up and down with the highs/lows of melodies
Science	Learn numbers by counting body parts	Feel the textures of different objects	Do a movement which helps to understand what happens during digestion

The MISP routine itself can also be used to create fairy tales, stories from the past, and legends from other countries. During the Massage In Schools Programme Instructors Course, Instructors receive various ideas about developing that aspect of the programme.

The following points will help clarify the descriptions of the above movements for school subjects.

Geography

- 4–6 years: Do the weather massage as described in Chapter 33. Touch Games.
- 7–9 years: Children can draw mountains, trees, and lakes, on each other's backs.
- 10–12 years: Have a child draw the shape of a country on the back of another child.

History

- 4–6 years: Have children act out characters of legends and local tales. The story can be read and the children can draw some of the elements of the story (for instance, if it was a King, they could draw the crown).
- 7–9 years: Have children draw their country's flag or emblem on each other's backs.
- 10–12 years: Have children get into small groups and pretend to create mummies, and the steps required for that activity.

Language

- 4–6 years: The child draws the form of a simple word (such as a star) on another child's back, who then guesses what word (i.e- form) was written (i.e. drawn)
- 7–9 years: This alphabet exercise develops a child's ability to focus. One child gently presses a hand on another child's back for one

second, and silently thinks the letters of the alphabet in order. The child presses one time for each letter, stopping at any letter of choice. The other child will also need to be reciting the alphabet silently in rhythm with the hand pressing. When the first child stops pressing, the second child names the letter of the alphabet.

- 10–12 years: The teacher says a word in one language and the child writes the foreign word on the back of another child.

Maths

- 4–6 years: The teacher says a simple number, and the child practises writing that number on another child's back.
- 7–9 years: Use soft fabric balls (as they do not roll). Have the children stand in a circle, and each child puts a ball in their left hand. Then all at the same time, they transfer the ball to their right hand, then back to their left hand, and finally into the right hand of the child on their left. As the child gives the ball to the child on their left, they receive a ball from the child on their right. The rhythm is: 2 x 1 is 2; 2x 2 is 4; 2 x 3 is 6; and so on. At the beginning the rhythm must be set by the teacher.
- 10–12 years: Geometric shapes can be done with all the children of the class holding hands, or putting their hands on each other's shoulders. It is very good for their neural connections to have them experiment with shapes in space.

Music

- 4–6 years: The children can sing a simple song and clap their hands or stamp their feet in time to the rhythm.
- 7–9 years: Sing songs like, "Head, Shoulders, Knees, and Toes" or "Give Your Friend a Massage" while doing the movements.
- 10–12 years: The teacher plays music and the children move their hands up or down, following on the highs and lows of the melody. Note: When we listen to music that is 60 beats/minute, our

heartbeat synchronizes with the beat of the music and our bodies relax. Our brain even gets into sync, producing more alpha and theta brainwaves, significantly improving our ability to learn. Largo, andante, and adagio movements, such as those in baroque and classical music with their regular beat, have a calming effect. Several pieces by Bach, Handel, Pachelbel, Mozart, and Vivaldi are all excellent for helping the brain and the body to be receptive to learning.

Science

- 4–6 years: The teacher says the different body parts that are related to numbers as the children either point to or wave the body parts around; for example, point to two eyes and wave ten fingers.
- 7–9 years: With their eyes closed, half of the children can be offered different types of textures by the other half of the children. They then feel the object with their hands and guess what they are touching (i.e. velvet, rocks, sandpaper, water, cotton balls, different fruits and vegetables, etc.). This helps the children to understand the efficiency of their skin receptors.
- 10–12 years: Have the children divide up into small groups representing: food, mouth, teeth, throat, stomach, small intestine, large intestine, and rectum. The food group goes into the mouth group first. A circle of children holding hands forms the mouth. Then the food is chewed. The teeth move up and down on the food. Then the food goes through the throat (the children make a long narrow passage). When the food arrives in the stomach, the children who make up the stomach churn the food back and forth; afterwards the food goes into the small intestines, which presses the food. The large intestine begins to squeeze the food, and eventually it goes through the rectum, which is made up of a group of three or four children forming a barrier for the food to get through.

Movement in conjunction with poetry or inspiring texts can be done at any time with any school subject. Stories and fairy tales can inspire teachers, who can use their own creativity to create forms to be moved on by all the children in the classroom.

33. Touch Games and Activities

"The role of imagination or the ability to think in images is recognized as an important component in creative thinking. Albert Einstein said he discovered the theory of relativity by picturing himself riding on a ray of light."

Rahima Baldwin

Teachers can use touch games any time during the day, and for many different reasons. Because they involve touch, they can have a calming effect on the children and can therefore be particularly useful if used directly after lunch or a break. They can be linked with a school curriculum subject, or they can be used to develop social skills amongst the children, or used just for fun or at the end of the school day. They can also be done during staff meetings, or during meetings when the parents are being informed about the programme. The Weather Massage (a detailed description follows) is an excellent tool for helping parents to better understand the value of using touch in school. The Weather Massage can easily be adapted in a variety of ways, such as adding volcanoes, earthquakes, or adjusting the story. Below are a few other variations of the Weather Massage which can also be done on the back:

- planting a garden
- baking a pizza
- singing a song like "Head, Shoulders, Knees, and Toes" or "Give Your Friend a Massage"
- being different animals walking through the forest (bear, tiger, mouse, etc.)

- telling fairy tales or stories through the movements ("We're going on a bear hunt...", "We're going to catch a big one...")

Parents can also use the ideas above, or by:

- telling a good-night story with the moon and stars
- telling a story with nocturnal animals
- letting the children make up their own stories

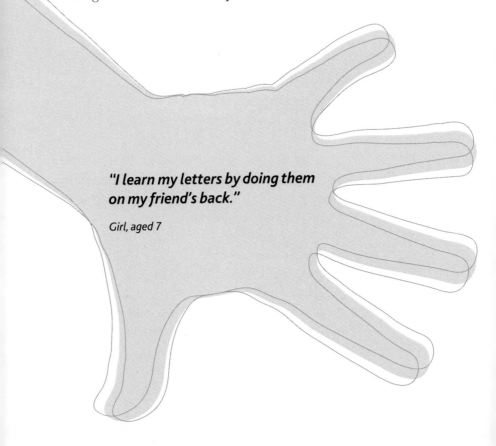

"I learn my letters by doing them on my friend's back."

Girl, aged 7

Weather Massage

Spoken words	Movements
"Once upon a time there was a big, yellow sun that warmed the whole earth.	With one hand on the shoulder, take the other hand and make a circle clockwise on the back.
And from the middle of the sun, sunrays reach out and touch all parts of the world.	Make sunrays to the sides.
But look! Clouds appear and cover the sun.	Make small circles with finger pads.
Then the wind comes and blows harder... and harder...and harder	Move hands from side to side.... harder and harder.
... until the wind turns into a tornado and a hurricane, and a typhoon.	Begin at shoulders, and make tornado-like strokes with finger pads.
Then comes lightning...	Make lightning with finger tips.
... and thunder.	Clap the back with hands.
Then comes the rain...	From the shoulders, stroke down with finger pads.
... and it rains harder and harder.	Same as above except faster and faster.
The rain turns into hail.	Play with finger tips on back.
The hail turns into snow, and everything is white and beautiful.	Press lightly with fingers slowly over back.
And the only thing you see is the cat that climbed up onto the roof of the house... and another cat... and a third cat.	Climb up toward neck by first using palm of hand, then rolling the hand upward, first up one side, then the middle of the back, then the other side.
The cats watch as a fog appears and everything becomes still... and quiet.	Lay hands still on the back. Begin at centre of back and slowly make a circle, getting bigger and bigger until the sun appears again.
Until the sun comes out and burns the fog away, and warms up the earth once again."	Begin at centre of back and slowly make a circle, getting bigger and bigger until the sun appears again.

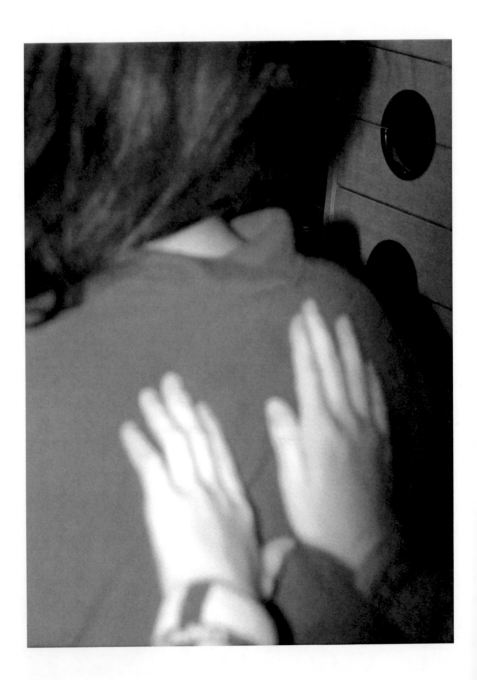

34. Special Situations

*"To say that the growing child is affected by
her environment is rather an understatement:
she is affected by the impressions of the world as deeply as she is
affected by the substance of the world...
Making sense of the world begins with the sense of touch."*

Martyn Rawson and Michael Rose

Teachers working with children who have special/additional needs often enquire as to whether the MISP is suitable for those children too. The answer, of course, is "yes"! Nurturing touch is for all children, without exception. Adaptations will probably need to be made both to the strokes and sometimes to the entire way the routine is performed, depending on the needs and capabilities of the child. Below are some special situations and ideas for dealing with them.

Children sensitive to touch

Some children exhibit evident behaviour of being sensitive to touch; they can be tactile defensive, or resistant to touch. This sensitivity must be respected. It is not the role of the MISP Instructor to find the causes of this behaviour; rather, the role of the Instructor is to support the child, and help find a touch or movement that works for that child.

Signs of resistance to touch can vary widely. Children who do not know how to use their body might not know how "hard" their touch is and therefore end up accidentally pushing other children. Other children, not knowledgeable about their physical boundaries, may appear very clumsy. Some children may tense up or become aggressive when touched. Others cannot bear to wear itchy clothes or clothes with tags; clothes can be too loose or tight; certain fabrics are unacceptable. These are just a few examples.

With these children, we may need to be extra patient and understand that at the outset they may refuse touch. This must be respected at all times. They may be more comfortable with very light pressure, or alternatively very firm pressure. A first approach to touch and massage can be to only rest your hands without moving them at all.

Children who say "no" to massage

This programme is all about respect, so it stands to reason that MISP Instructors and school teachers must allow a child the right to say "no" to massage. However, in these situations, it is important to have the child stay in the classroom. Have the child sit down and just watch. Some children simply need to observe before feeling secure enough to participate in something new. Some children have never experienced safe positive touch before, and need to get used to the idea. It may even be that on a specific day, a child does not feel like being massaged; most of us feel that way from time to time. Not forcing the child, but allowing the child to get used to the idea of massage, often helps the child to start to relax and accept the idea of being massaged.

It does not usually take long, however, before the child wants to join the group being massaged. Perhaps it is in part due to the combined effect of oxytocin and other relaxing hormones that start circulating in the room. Or perhaps, they just see and feel that their classmates are enjoying the massage. Always respect the child and allow the desire to be massaged to grow of itself. Forcing never helps.

Children unable to massage

Some children with special/additional needs lack the motor skills to be able to give a massage. This can range from having a lack of some motor skills to being paralysed. If a child has limited motor skills, perhaps the child can do something with the assistance of simple massage tools, such as: small wooden or plastic tools with handles and wheels or rollers. Some are well designed, and the educator can look for one that a child can grip easily. These children feel a lot of satisfaction when they are able to give, even if it is just a little and with a tool instead of their hands.

It may be possible and appropriate to assist a child in giving a massage by placing a hand on top of the child's hand and gently guiding the child in doing the massage. In such a case, the only adults allowed to touch the child are those who know the child, who already work with that child, and who are legally allowed to include touch in their care of the child.

Hyperactivity and Attention Deficit Disorder

The terms Attention Deficit Disorder and Attention Deficit Hyperactivity Disorder point to profound challenges within the educational realm. It is not the purpose of this book to explain or try to identify possible causes. What can be said, however, is that such behaviourally challenged children seem to make gains and to cope better as a result of the MISP.

The MISP is certainly not a cure; however, it is one tool, amongst others, which can aid the child in coping with and more effectively managing their hyperactivity.

Cultural habits

Children from various cultures may have certain restrictions with regard to being massaged. Such restrictions must be respected. The benefit is that it creates an opportunity for other children to learn about other cultures, as well as helping to inculcate a sense of respect.

Head lice

Head lice constitute a special situation that may arise in a classroom, or in an entire school. Removing the head strokes from the MISP routine because of the possibility of head lice was considered at one point. However, there was a great deal of positive feedback on the head massage – for example, the discovery of different hair textures. Therefore, it was decided to leave the head strokes in the MISP routine, and the decision as to whether to avoid the head massage because of head lice would be left up to the teachers and head teachers in each specific situation.

Children and hygiene

A child who is particularly dirty, has dirty hands, or who is smelly can become a special case in the classroom, and can have a direct impact on the smooth running of the programme. Such issues can be complex, and go beyond the MISP Instructor's role. Schools must work in close liaison with social workers and school nurses in extreme situations. However, when a quick solution is needed, one that is commonly used by Instructors and school teachers is to have unscented wet wipes, with which children can clean their hands (and faces) before performing the routine. The cost is minimal, and it is effective. It can assist the child in developing a habit of cleanliness, and help to ensure that all the children are involved.

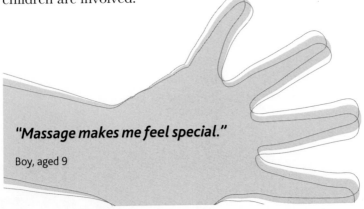

"Massage makes me feel special."

Boy, aged 9

"It's OK. Sometimes uncomfortable.

I do not always like people touching me."

Girl, aged 11

35. Especially for Parents

"There are parents… who are defying the directives of their culture. Such parents are not only helping their children to have a childhood…Those parents will help to keep alive a human tradition. [Our culture] is halfway toward forgetting that children need childhood. Those who insist on remembering shall perform a noble service."

Neil Postman

Although the Massage in Schools Programme was designed for the school set-up, massage does not only belong there. The effects of massage are not reserved only for massage-therapy clients, or for parents and babies in infant massage classes. Although massage can be therapeutic, massage is before anything else about nurturing touch. The value of massage has been demonstrated in this book, and we now encourage all parents to consider how the principles might also be applicable within family life.

A parent taking time to massage a child will contribute to reducing the child's stress, enhancing their relationship, and helping to raise the child's self-esteem. Children who participate in the Massage In Schools Programme at school will often do it spontaneously with their parents in the evening.

Before massaging your child, you can use your intuition, use ideas from this and/or other books on baby/child massage, or contact an MISP Instructor. Instructors also run classes for parents and children in the community, or teach the strokes to the parents at the child's school.

Here are some ideas for practising massage with your child:

- Always ask permission.
- You can massage over clothes or on bare skin.
- If you massage skin to skin, respect the child's modesty; leave underwear on and avoid body parts related to sexuality.
- If you massage skin to skin, use unscented, pure cold-pressed vegetable oil, such as sunflower or olive oil. Added perfumes can be over-stimulating for some children.
- If you want to use essential oils, use mandarin, which is the only one that is recognized as having a balancing effect on children. (The effect of essential oils on adults is very different than it is on children, and sometimes even has the opposite effect. Essential oils need to be used with the help of knowledgeable aromatherapists who have experience in working with children.)
- Work with your child's cues. Ask them what they like and dislike, and adjust the pressure or strokes according to their preferences.
- Link massage with your child's specific interests and/or heroes. You can call the massage a sports massage, a climber's massage, a dancer's massage, and so on.
- Do touch games as suggested in this book. They are easy, and they encourage your child's imagination.
- Ask your child to massage you.
- Have a family massage gathering, where everyone massages one another's feet or shoulders while sitting on the sofa or listening to music.
- Give your child a shoulder massage during a break from homework.

Remember to have fun!

If massage finds its way into family, school, and work situations, we will all find that the world is a good place to be, after all!

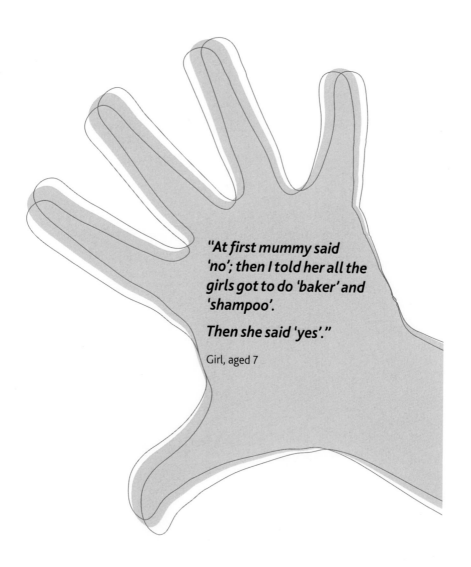

"At first mummy said 'no'; then I told her all the girls got to do 'baker' and 'shampoo'.

Then she said 'yes'."

Girl, aged 7

36. Comments and Observations from Parents

"Have a heart that never hardens,
and a temper that never tires,
and a touch that never hurts."

Charles Dickens

"When my child comes home from school, I get a massage. Nothing is better than 4-year-old hands!" Dad

"When massage came to our school, I was very sceptical, but after just one week I noticed a big difference in my son." Mum

"My son often had fights on the playground. While it occasionally still happens, he seems less aggressive and happier." Mum

"We are involved in a Saturday programme with massage. It gives me a special time to be with my little girl." Dad

"I pay my 7-year old grandchild 50p to give me a massage." Grandmother

"Initially, we said 'no' to our daughter participating in this activity. Eventually, we saw that she was upset about not getting to be involved. When we spoke with the teacher and Instructors, we understood that our daughter had the right to say 'yes' or 'no', and we immediately felt better about it." Parents

"My son is in a special-needs class that is integrated in the school. His class learned the massage first, and they, together with the Instructor and teachers, implemented it in the rest of the school. My son's self-esteem grew, because this was something he could teach to the 'normal' children, and those children have a different attitude about my son." Mum

"We are moving to another continent for a year, and I'm taking the Instructors Course, so I can implement it in their school. Then my 6-year-old daughter will have at least one thing that is familiar in her surroundings." Mum

"We have strict religious beliefs around touch. Our daughter is respected when she says 'no' to certain parts of the routine, and is not made to feel like an outsider." Parents

"My youngest daughter engaged our entire family of six in doing massage, and often we spend a few minutes together doing the massage when we get home from school and work." Mum

"When my sons give each other a massage, they don't fight. At least, for the duration of the massage." Mum

"My granddaughter asks me to do the Weather Massage on her back. If I forget something, or do it in the wrong order, she reminds me. There is no way I could possibly leave anything out!" Grandmother

"When we were on holidays, the coach driver complained of a headache and our 4-year-old son said, 'I could give you a massage and it would make you feel better'." Mum

"I wish everything my child did at school was this useful." Parent's comment after receiving a massage

"At first I was a little bit scared about massage, but I fully trust our teacher and I have seen my child opening up and telling us more about what he was doing at school, things he wouldn't tell us before." Parent

"Our son now does everything possible to get to school before registration. He doesn't want to miss a second of morning massage." Parents

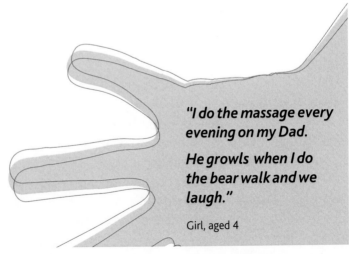

"I do the massage every evening on my Dad.

He growls when I do the bear walk and we laugh."

Girl, aged 4

163

Rubbing the right way
to help the school day

37. Beyond Reward and Punishment

"Habit formation makes punishment superfluous."

Freya Jaffke

Hopefully, everyone who reads this book is now convinced of the importance of touch for the healthy development of children and for human beings in general.

Changes are only made when people are convinced that change is necessary. Necessity and understanding will hopefully breed the inspiration to create environments and develop habits that bring healthy touch into the lives of children, both at school and at home.

Touch is as important as food for all human beings. Therefore, all adults who implement the principles of massage in the lives of the children around them are urged never to use a massage routine as a reward or as a punishment. A child who misbehaves or loses control is a child that can be helped by massage.

Massage or touch games should become part of children's lives, exactly as meals are part of their lives. Remember that routines have a calming effect on children. They bring an inner security that helps a child to take steps forward in life. Establish a rhythm with the activities, and ensure that all the children do them.

So-called good or bad behaviour should never be linked to having or not having a massage. Massage is a tool. If children are asked to do something or to be a certain way in order to be entitled to receive nurturing touch, they will experience extra inner pressure, which is something that should be reduced, not increased.

Early in the development of the MISP, a teacher in a school was only using massage with the children who behaved badly. One day, a little girl from the class went home and told her parents, "It doesn't matter how quiet I am or how well behaved I am. I raise my hand. I do my work. But I never get massage". That was an important lesson. By giving massage only to badly behaved children, the teacher was unwittingly promoting bad behaviour. It is logical that children might subconsciously think that being naughty would entitle them to massage.

Another subconscious thought that a child who is behaviourally challenged might have is that they are not worthy, which in turn might promote even more negative behaviour. The MISP now makes it clear that the routine is for nurturing touch, and is not to be used as either a reward or a punishment.

Managing behaviour should not be linked with a massage routine. Embrace the idea that a regular massage has positive benefits for the child, and these benefits go beyond personality, character, and behaviour.

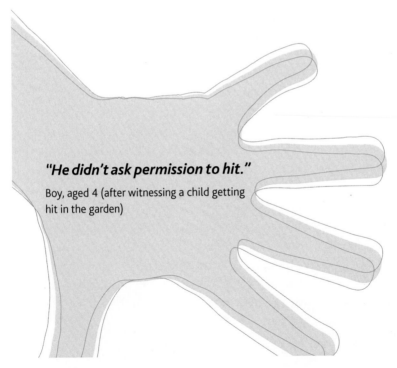

"He didn't ask permission to hit."
Boy, aged 4 (after witnessing a child getting hit in the garden)

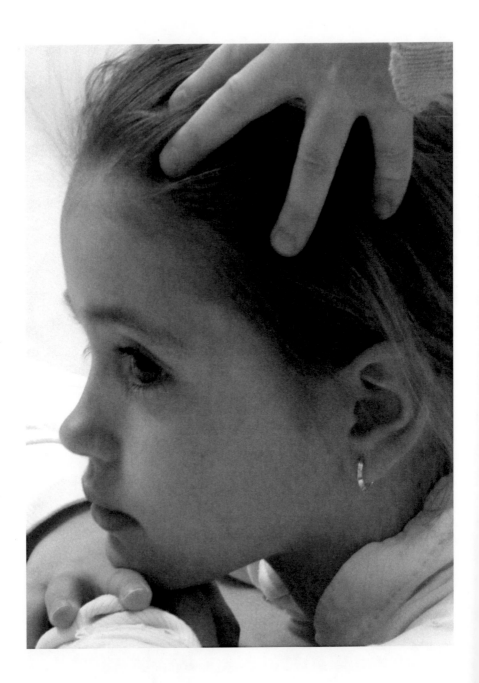

38. The Next Step

"Many schools today are a battleground. Teachers are overstressed and underpaid; kids have less and less socialisation from home (good manners, calm influences, feeling wanted and loved)... The classroom becomes a battle for survival with only two goals – getting the girls to achieve and the boys to behave.."

Steve Biddulph

Here at the end of this book, we are calling for involvement. What to do with all the information gained from *Touch in Schools*?

Joseph Chilton Pearce states, in the foreword, that if he were younger, he would give time and energy to this "cause". We are so grateful that he DID give time and energy to read the whole book and support it, and now we call for everyone who is "touched" by the book to take action. If, in your core, you feel that this is valuable, then we invite you to take the necessary steps to ensure that all the children you know start to benefit from the programme as soon as possible, both within the school system and within their family life. YOUR involvement counts. We would like to express our gratitude to all who are dedicated to spreading the word about the MISP approach. Your dedication makes it possible for thousands of children to experience safe, healthy, and nurturing touch as part of their daily life. That is a sure step toward a world where more love blooms and flows.

Sylvie Hétu

Mia Elmsäter

The Authors

The Massage In Schools Programme (MISP), as presented in this book, is the co-creation of the authors and founders of the programme, **MIA ELMSÄTER** and **SYLVIE HÉTU**. Under the International Association of Infant Massage (IAIM), both have been Instructors since the 1980s, and Instructor Trainers since 1989 (Sylvie) and 1990 (Mia).

As members of the Education Committee of IAIM, they educate Instructors and train Trainers globally. Together and independently they have created films and various programmes to support parent educators, teachers, and older children, as well as parents and babies.

Stemming from their pioneering work with infant massage in their respective countries (Mia in Sweden and Sylvie in Canada), there were extended requests for adapting this programme for various ages and situations. There were invitations to teach toddler groups, massage in day-care centres, pre-schools, schools, and in nursing homes, as well as to give lectures and workshops to teachers in conferences, colleges, and universities.

With the founders' combined passion, vast experience, and training in education, including Steiner, Montessori, and mainstream approaches, a very solid foundation of expertise and experience underpins the programme. The Massage in Schools Programme, which began in the UK in 2000, is now being implemented on six continents.

Both Mia and Sylvie have three children.

Bibliography

Ackerman, Diane. *Sinnenas naturlära.* Trans. Margareta Eklöf. Stockholm, Sweden: Forum AB, 1993. (Original title: *A Natural History of the Senses.* 1990).

Anschütz, Marieke. *Children and their Temperaments.* Edinburgh, UK: Floris Books, 1995.

Aron, Elaine. *The Highly Sensitive Child: Helping Our Children Thrive When the World Overwhelms Them.* London, UK: Thorsons, 2002.

Ayres, Jean. *Sensory Integration and the Child.* Los Angeles, CA, USA: Western Psychological Services, 2005.

Berron, Joachim. *Sept regards sur l'enfance.* Montreal, Canada: Edition DGP, 1999.

Birkestad, Gunilla. *Beröring i vård och omsorg.* Solna, Sweden: Ófeigur förlag, 1999.

Björkqvist, Karin. *Harmoni i klassen.* Göteborg, Sweden: Skapande Hälsa, 2001.

Bowlby, Sir Richard. *Fifty Years of Attachment Theory.* London, UK: Karnac Books, 2004.

Boyd, Gary. Education for ecological viability through co-operative action. In V. Nolan and G. Darby (eds), *Reinventing Education: A 'Thought Experiment'.* Stoke Mandeville, UK: Synectics Education Initiative, Bucks, 2005, pp. 213-23.

Britz-Crecelius, Heidi. *Children at Play: Using Waldorf Principles to Foster Childhood Development.* Rochester, VT, USA: Inner Traditions International, 1996.

Brody, Viola A. *The Dialogue of Touch, Development Play Therapy,* 2nd edn. Northvale, NJ, USA, Jason Aronson, 1997.

Buscaglia, Leo. *Living, Loving, and Learning.* New York, NY, USA: Ballantine Books, 1983.

Caplan, Mariana, *To Touch is to Live.* Third Eye, Prescott, AZ, USA, 2005.

Dolto, Françoise. *Les Etapes Majeuures de L'Enfance.* Paris, France: Gallimard, 1998.

Elkind, David. *Miseducation - Preschoolers at Risk.* New York, USA: Alfred A. Knopf, 1996.

Ellersiek Wilma. *Giving Love: Bringing Joy, Hand Gesture Games, and Lullabies in the Mood of the Fifth.* Spring Valley, NY, USA: Waldorf Early Childhood Association of North America (WECAN), 2003.

Ellneby, Ylva. *Om du inte rör mig så dör jag.* Stockholm, Sweden: Utbildningsradion, 1994.

Field, Tiffany. *Touch.* Cambridge, MA, USA: MIT Press, 2003.

Frommer, Eva A. *Voyage through Childhood into the Adult World.* Stroud, UK: Hawthorn Press, 1994.

Gardner, Howard. *Frames of Mind: The Theory of Multiple Intelligences.* New York, NY, USA: Basic Books, 1993.

Gardner, Howard. *Intelligence Reframed: Multiple Intelligences for the 21st Century.* New York, NY, USA: Basic Books, 1999.

Gardner, Howard. *Multiple Intelligences: The Theory in Practice.* New York, NY, USA: Basic Books, 1993.

Gerhardt, Sue. *Why Love Matters: How Affection Shapes a Baby's Brain.* Hove, UK: Brunner-Routledge, 2004.

Goddard, Sally. *Reflexes, Learning and Behavior: A Window into the Child's Mind.* Eugene, OR, USA: Fern Ridge Press, 2002.

Goddard Blythe, Sally. *The Well Balanced Child: Movement and Early Learning.* Stroud, UK: Hawthorn Press, 2004.

Goleman, Daniel. *Emotional Intelligence: Why It Can Matter More than IQ.* London, UK: Bloomsbury, 1996.

Gudmundsson, Christer. *Lär med musik.* 2nd edn. Jönköping, Sweden: Brain Books, 1997.

Gunzenhauser, Nina (ed.). *Advances in Touch: New Implications in Human Touch.* Key Biscayne, FL, USA: Johnson and Johnson Consumer Products, 1990.

Haller, Ingerborg. *How Children Play.* Edinburgh, UK: Floris Books, 1991.

Hannaford, Carla. *Smart Moves: Why Learning Is Not All in Your Head.* Alexander, NC, USA: Great Ocean Publishers, 1995.

Healy, Jane M. *Endangered Minds: Why Children Don't Think and What to Do about It.* New York, NY, USA: Touchstone/Simon & Schuster, 1991.

Hétu, Sylvie. *The Song of the Child.* London, UK and Montreal, Canada: UR Publications and Programmes, 2004.

Honoré, Carl. *In Praise of Slow: How a Worldwide Movement Is Challenging the Cult of Speed.* London, UK: Orion, 2004.

hooks, bell. *All about Love.* London, UK: The Women's Press, 2001.

Hughes, Daniel. A. *Building the Bonds of Attachment: Awakening Love in Deeply Troubled Children.* Northvale, NJ, USA: Jason Aronson, 1998.

Jaffke, Freya. *Work and Play in Early Childhood.* Edinburgh, UK: Floris Books, 2000.

Jelvéus, Lena. *Berör mig! – Massage för små och stora barn.* Stockholm, Sweden: Utbildningsradion, 1998.

Klaus, Marshall H., Kennel, John H., & Klaus, Phyllis H. *Bonding: Building the Foundations of Secure Attachment and Independence.* Reading, MA, USA: Addison-Wesley, 1995.

Koepke, Herman. *Encountering the Self.* New York, NY, USA: Anthroposophic Press, 1989.

Köhler, Henning. *Les enfants agités, anxieux, tristes.* Montesson, France: Editions Novalis, 1995.

Korczak, Januz. *A Voice for the Child.* Trans. Sandra Joseph. London, UK: Thorsons, 1999.

Kuhlewind, Georg. *Les enfants "étoiles".* Paris, France: Triades, 2002.

Liedloff, Jean. *The Continuum Concept.* London, UK: Penguin, 2004 (orig.1975).

Lievegoed, Bernard. *Phases de l'Enfance.* Chatou, France: Les Trois Arches. 1993.

McClure, Vimala Schneider. *Infant Massage – A Handbook for Loving Parents.* New York, NY, USA: Bantam Books, 2001.

Masheder, Mildred. *Let's Play Together: Over 300 Co-operative Games for Children and Adults.* Woodbridge, Suffolk, UK: Green Print/Merlin Press, 1989.

Mellon, Nancy. *Storytelling with Children.* Stroud, UK: Hawthorn Press, 2000.

Meyer, Rudolf. *The Wisdom of Fairy Tales,* 2nd edn. Edinburgh, UK: Floris Books, 1997.

Moberg, Kerstin Uvnäs. *Lugn och Beröring.* Stockholm, Sweden: Natur and Kultur, 2000.

Moberg, Kerstin Uvnäs. *The Oxytocin Factor: Tapping the Hormone of Calm, Love, and Healing.* Cambridge, MA, USA: Da Capo Press, 2003.

Montagu, Ashley. *Touching – The Human Significance of the Skin,* 3rd edn. New York, NY, USA: Harper & Row, 1986.

Pearce, Joseph Chilton. *Magical Child.* New York, NY, USA. Plume Printing, 1992 (orig.1977).

Rawson, Martyn & Michael Rose. *Ready to Learn: From Birth to School Readiness.* Stroud, UK: Hawthorn Press, 2002.

Reivich, Karen & Shatté, Andrew. *The Resilience Factor: Seven Keys to Finding Your Inner Strengths and Overcoming Life's Hurdles.* New York, NY, USA: Broadway Books, 2002.

Ruiz, Don Miguel. *The Four Agreements: A Practical Guide to Personal Freedom.* San Rafael, CA, USA: Amber-Allen Publishing, Inc., 1997.

Schwartz, Eugene. *Millennial Child: Transforming Education in the Twenty-first Century.* Hudson, NY, USA: Anthroposophic Press, 1999.

Soesman, Albert. *Our Twelve Senses.* Stroud, UK: Hawthorn Press, 1990.

Sunderland, Margot. *Using Story Telling as a Therapeutic Tool with Children.* Bicester, Oxon, UK: Winslow Press, 2000.

Sunderland, Margot. *The Science of Parenting.* London, UK: Dorling Kindersley, 2006.

van Houten, Coenraad. *Awakening the Will.* London, UK: Temple Lodge, 1999.

Ward, Christine & Jan Daley. *Learning to Learn: Strategies for Accelerating Learning and Boosting Performance.* Christchurch, New Zealand: Caxton Press, 1998.

Wilkinson, Roy & Rudolf Steiner. *Education: A Compendium.* Stroud, UK: Hawthorn Press, 1993.

Winn, Marie. *The Plug-In Drug: Television, Computers, and Family Life.* New York, NY, USA: Penguin Books, 1977, rev. 2002.

Index

UR
Publications &
Programmes Inc.

www.urpublications.com

PROGRAMMES

Massage in Schools Programme

hands-on respect

www.massageinschools.com

The programme, about which you have learned in this book *Touch in Schools*, is now present (on the date of writing, mid-January 2010) in some twenty countries/territories on every continent.

Please visit our website to find an instructor in your region.

Working Together with Consensus

Available for any organization/association/company members wanting to learn the principles of true consensus work and the revolutionary structural aspects that lie behind it.

International Implementing

A programme designed for any person, business, or organization wishing to expand internationally. Includes the cultural dimension, thus fostering the successful unfolding of new initiatives abroad.

BOOKS

The Song of the Child by Sylvie Hétu

A richly artistic treasure house of imaginative, poetic insights for retrieving the deep mystery that is "the child", and bringing it to our adult awareness. Illustrated with beautiful watercolour paintings.